widow—
widower—
widowest—

a grief mosaic

aaron m. simmons
polly g. simmons

Text copyright © 2026 by Aaron M. Simmons and Polly G. Simmons
All rights reserved. Printed in the United States of America
Published by Motina Books, LLC, Bailey, CO
www.MotinaBooks.com

Library of Congress Cataloguing-in-Publication Data
Names: Simmons, Aaron M. and Simmons, Polly G.
Title: widow— widower— widowest—
Description: First Edition. | Bailey, CO Motina Books, 2026

Identifiers:
LCCN: 2025943440

ISBN-13: 979-8-88784-065-9 (hardcover)
ISBN-13: 979-8-88784-063-5 (ebook)
ISBN-13: 979-8-88784-064-2 (paperback)

Subjects:
BIOGRAPHY & AUTOBIOGRAPHY / Memoirs
FAMILY & RELATIONSHIPS / Death, Grief, Bereavement
FAMILY & RELATIONSHIPS / Marriage & Long-Term Relationships

Excerpt from *What Doesn't Kill Us* by Stephen Joseph, copyright (c) 2011.
Reprinted by permission of Basic Books, an imprint of Hachette Book Group, Inc.

For Polly.
I carry you with me.

to find the words i haven't said— to the man i
haven't met— about the mother he'll never meet—
... tomorrow i'll have the courage— to say, "help—
help me— i need— i can't do this alone"— i can't
do this alone— i won't have to do this alone—

—from an untitled poem by Polly
(probably written in college)

expectations cause suffering—

—Polly's aphorism

Table of Contents

Foreword

After my wife Polly died, we wrote a book together. In the process I discovered that we were both writers.

I still hesitate to use that word for myself. But then I remember a moment with Polly, back when we first met, sitting on a balcony in Sagada, Philippines. She was smoking, and I was still surprised that it wasn't a turn-off. (In fact, it was incredibly sexy.) She wasn't convinced she was a smoker. "But maybe," she said, taking a drag and trying out an idea, "someone who smokes is a smoker."

Ergo, what is someone who writes?

Everyone thought I was going to be a writer after I published a little novelette in high school. I was going to be the *Eragon* guy. ("It's great... for a fifteen-year-old.") But then I hit a wall. I didn't have anything to write *about*. Also, writing is hard, and programming computers is easier. A computer will tell you if you did it right (even if sloppily), but people will disagree about your writing. So the writer got buried under sedimentary layers of engineering and went to sleep.

Polly's death was like an acid bath, dissolving away layer after layer, seemingly everything. At the bottom the writer was still there, and he woke up. The writing started with Polly's eulogy and just kept going. I'm not sure if I have anything to write about other than Polly and our family ("write what you know"), but the writer is awake now. We'll see what happens.

On the other hand, Polly presented herself as an artist, not a writer. While she would proudly show off her art, she never really talked about writing or showed me much of it. I think her writer got buried, too. She'd also hit the wall:

> it seems i still want to write but i have nothing to say— that's really my problem— even if i conceive a plot line i don't know what else to do with it— i can't think of any plot lines right now— how about a character description—

Is having nothing to say in your twenties really so surprising? What's really surprising is that someone in their twenties would have the chutzpah to think they have something to say. (Maybe that's what separates the real writers from whatever it is I'm doing.)

But unlike me, Polly never stopped writing:

*hell, i never practice anything— so, i want to
write— write, then—*

And she did. In her journal, in the corners of her sketchbooks, in piles of computer docs all "Untitled." Mostly undated, in an unbroken stream, almost all in her idiosyncratic style, sort of like e.e. cummings with dashes. (Rendered here in a font she made from her own handwriting.)

About her style, she says:

*the dash is important in my work as the
primary form of punctuation— the dash has a
rather ambiguous place in the gamut of
punctuation— to me, it is like a slur in
musical notation— a deliberate blurring of
meaning between phrases— it is a pause, a
breath—*

She wrote nearly every day about whatever was on her mind, often in a poetic mode, often in the second person. I'm usually the "you," though it varies.

What a gift. How did I not know she was a writer? She kept it to herself, though there were clues. We were always batting around story ideas. It was a sort of game.

In the last year of her life, when she was trying to clear space to be something other than a stay-at-home mom, Polly said she wanted to write a book. (To my everlasting shame, I didn't take the book goal seriously at first.) I don't know what it was going to be about. I'm not sure

Polly did. All I know is that she hefted up her box of old journals into our little office and was going to go through them. Perhaps she was going to write a memoir. Perhaps she was going to write a grief mosaic about her mom. Now in her forties, she'd lived through more experiences (three kids, a thirteen-year marriage, time in the Peace Corps) and she finally had something to say.

Polly was going to start just as soon as she recovered from the surgery.

This book, a mosaic of our "found" writings blended together, is my last gift to her, our last collaboration. Polly, you were a writer, and now everyone can see it.

Widower?

Polly Jo Simmons died unexpectedly of a pulmonary embolism the morning of October 23, 2022. She is survived by her husband, Aaron Michael Simmons, and her three children: Peggy Jo Simmons (11), Hazel Maude Simmons (8) and Cary Jay Simmons (5). She was preceded in death by her mother, Nancy Jo Cooper Gates, who died when Polly was 18.

Polly was born on March 17, 1979 to Samuel Bartlett Gates and Nancy Jo Cooper Gates. She was the youngest of three—her older brothers are Rudd and Joel.

Born and raised in Lakewood, Colorado, she graduated from Lakewood High School. She earned a Bachelor's of Fine Arts followed by a Master's of Fine Arts from the University of Colorado Boulder.

After college and a stint at the Post Office, Polly served in the Peace Corps for two years in the Philippines, teaching art and English at Besao National High School.

While in the Peace Corps, she met Aaron. When they got back to the States, Polly and Aaron married at the Denver Museum of Nature and Science (under the foot of the giant T-Rex fossil) on Feb 6, 2010. They settled down in Boulder, Colorado to start a family.

Polly was an artist in every moment, every thought—in everything she did. And always there was color, color, and more color. She couldn't stop making things. There was always a project in the works that would be infused with her aesthetic, elevating the mundane, from painted wall patterns to custom-built furniture to funny custom T-shirts to a redesigned bathroom to collaborating with her kids on a painting. She wasn't bound to a single medium—the world was her canvas. Our lives were her canvas.

A Celebration of Life will be held Sunday, December 11, 2022 at the Boulder Museum of Contemporary Art (BMoCA). The celebration will begin at 1pm with a service, followed by hearty appetizers, beer and wine in a gallery setting full of Polly's art. While our hearts are heavy with grief, we wish to truly celebrate the vibrant, independent, colorful person Polly Jo Simmons will always be to us. *Please do not wear black.* We encourage elegant, bohemian-chic, and colorful attire.

—the ultimate test
of one's values—

parenting— that ultimate test of one's values— pick
nose— what?— to wipe or to eat?— my kids have a book
about noses— it matter of factly points out that boogers
are dirty— i guess insinuating that one shouldn't eat
what's dirty— and, okay, i'm a fan of kleenex, tissues,
hankies, whatever— but what about when you don't have
one?— maybe you should have thought about that when you
picked your nose— sure— but you didn't— so, the
dilemma— to wipe or to eat— i recently discovered that
my eldest was wiping— on the wall— on the furniture—
now, i clean our house— it's my job— so i have a given
perspective— not a fan of scratching, scrubbing off
other people's hardened boogers— and, yes, my
preference is eating— yes, boogers are dirty— by

design— but the design is to keep the dirt out of our lungs— not our stomachs— do you know how much snot a person typically swallows in a day?— me neither, but i bet it's a lot— we should look it up— it's a lot right?— because our stomach can handle it— it's full of acid— it was made to handle dirt— so, okay, boogers are dirty— and you know where they're really dirty?— on the goddamn wall— i'm not saying we should go ahead and go to town in front of people— it's okay to be a little sneaky— but please, if you don't have a tissue— eat those filthy motherfuckers— so, parenting— the ultimate test of one's values— values you didn't even know you had— now i've set it up— i don't know which option is grosser— well, all things being equal, makes sense to please myself— eat booger— and that's my rant today— my little standup—

The Vestments of My Office

I still wear my wedding ring.

Once, I took it off briefly to do some messy food prep in the kitchen. I put it in the little ceramic bowl above the sink, like Polly used to do. (She was always taking her wedding ring off to do messy things, and not just kitchen stuff. Painting, carpentry, gardening, cement-mixing by hand, who-knows-what. But she didn't want to misplace it, so she had the little bowl.)

My finger felt stark and naked. The opposite of how it felt when I was first wearing it after we were married. I remember it driving me *bananas* and I would constantly mess with it. But after a few weeks I got used to it, and it seemed strange not to have it on. Is that a metaphor for being married?

A voice in the back of my mind—that mix of technically-correct pragmatism and inner critic—said,

"You don't have to put this back on. What's it for, anyway?"

The question floated there. Why do I wear my wedding ring?

It's because I'm still married to her. She's not my ex-wife, she's my late wife.

(What is she "late" for, by the way? Did she miss an appointment? Why are all the death words so odd?)

The ring also functions as a kind of ward. This is not an eligible bachelor, ladies. The school counselor invited me to a recurring meeting of single parents so they could bond over how hard it is and trade tips and coping strategies. I don't know if the horror I felt showed in my face, but I demurred as politely as I could. A room full of single moms. You just know it would be 80% women, most of them divorced but probably some Hot Widows also. A room where they would know the ring was a lie, a little metal shield. No, no way.

I rushed to finish up and quickly washed my hands and got the ring back on. Phew.

"I should make you a shirt that says *Proud To Be Pussy-Whipped*," Polly said in her characteristic deadpan, in that way you couldn't quite tell if she was joking or serious. Sometimes it was both.

We had been going through a rough patch. With our youngest turning five and starting kindergarten, it was a moment to change how we were doing things. It had taken Polly a while to articulate what was wrong, and I had been frustrated and we'd argued as we slowly figured it out. Making it more complicated, we were having to learn how to argue. We had agreed on so many things for so long that our arguing skills had atrophied, if we'd ever had them.

I was coming around. She had been reading books about the gender imbalance in domestic labor, and there was one scheme in particular that seemed like it would work. "Let's go for it," I told her.

Was she proud of me? Or just relieved? As she often did, Polly turned a compliment into teasing, poking right at the heart of the difficulty of an endeavor like rebalancing who does what in the home. Men can be *really* fragile about this sort of thing, where there's even the hint of emasculation. I have less of this than some, but it's still in there. It's something I have to work against.

But the idea of wearing a shirt with the word "pussy" on it... I wasn't sure I could do it. It was embarrassing! I wonder, would I be as uncomfortable if her idea was a dick joke? Maybe. I was never one to parade around in one of those dumb "Big Johnson" T-shirts, though I have to admit I would probably be uncomfortable more because of the frat connotations than with the dick joke itself. Jokey male euphemisms are normalized in a way that we don't tend to think about, but if you wear a pussy hat, get ready for some attention.

Polly never got around to making the shirt. After she died, her joke popped into my head. I realized that not only did I need to make this shirt, I needed to wear it. But when?

Polly's birthday is St. Patrick's Day. I'd like to think it

would have occurred to me while she was alive, but it would have been hilarious to order a green shirt with "Proud To Be Pussy-Whipped" on it in pink letters and just put it on the morning of her birthday. It would be like calling her bluff. Would she notice? Would she laugh? I loved hearing her laugh.

So when her birthday came around, five months after she died, that's what I did. I sat next to her ashes and I put on the shirt and I imagined what she would have said and I imagined her laughter. And then I wore the shirt outside, my face flushed, trying not to be embarrassed. I wore it all day, on a walk, to restaurants, meeting up with her friends.

My neighbor clapped when she saw it. Polly's friends loved it. At the coffee shop, the dude-bro cashier said, after I explained the shirt, "Is your wife, like, *intense*?" I plan on wearing it on her birthday from now on.

The funniest part of the joke is that I *am* proud. Proud to be, well, *you know…*

They handed me the box of her ashes. I was not prepared for the physicality of it, so small and oddly heavy. I held her in my arms, hugging her. Holding her ashes was like cradling a baby, but from the wrong end of her life. She was small, and fragile. *Don't drop her.* Overwhelmed, I sat down on the stairs and pulled her close.

It wasn't until the next day that I realized I'd forgotten to ask for her things. You know, her *things*. What she had been wearing when they took her. In particular, her wedding ring.

My sister-in-law called the mortuary. There were no things. She had been cremated in her pajamas. (No one had asked me what she should wear, and my brain was too broken to think of it on my own.) We called the first responders. There was no ring.

Ok, *breathe*, I told myself. My brain might've been compromised, but I could still think straight if I put in some effort. I could be a detective. *Let's think this through.* I could start with assuming these are professionals and not jump to conclusions that they misplaced or stole anything.

Given that assumption, where could her ring possibly be? Wait, there was something about surgeries and jewelry, wasn't there? They don't like you to wear jewelry. That's right, I had heard that before.

What if she took off her ring the morning of the surgery? After she got home, the recovery process took priority. Maybe she just never got around to putting it back on.

What a good story, but there was no ring on her bedside table. *Think.* How did that fit?

There… was a place for her jewelry, wasn't there? A jewelry box. Where was that? One of the drawers in the bathroom I never use—a memory of a blue box.

I went to the bathroom. I opened the drawer. I took out the blue box. I opened the blue box. There were little cubbies holding earrings, baubles, necklaces.

Rings.

There it was, right where she left it. Completely rational. She planned ahead. She wanted it to be safe.

I took her ring to the jewelry store we bought it from. Every year, she would make a point to go there and get her ring cleaned. I asked the clerk if they could clean our two rings.

While I waited, I listened to the customers. Women, excited to be engaged. Men, nervous to risk proposal. The circle of life, here in this jewelry store, but I'm at the wrong end.

I looped her newly cleaned ring through the chain. I pulled the chain over my head and around my neck. I could feel the weight of it there, like a metaphor for grief. I hold it sometimes, as a lifeline, when I can't remember if she's dead or not. I have a hard time taking it off.

I carry her with me.

Polly had a little abstract dark green lizard tattoo on the inside of her left heel, right under the ankle bone. Possibly a gecko, though her brothers teased her that it looked like a bit of barbed wire. I think it was her first tattoo; it had become smudgy with age. She had other tattoos: a turquoise Möbius strip between her shoulder blades (from her grad school "infinity woman" alter ego); a pink lowercase "i" on her upper right ribs (for the imaginary number, the square root of negative one).

The evening before her surgery, we had a long, liminal, close conversation late into the night. The weekend had been tense with all of our anticipation, and we'd argued. She was trying to feel close to me, and I realized that I had been spiky because of worry, and I melted. We talked and talked.

We had our feet up, and her tattoo was right there.

"I'm thinking of getting four more little geckos around it," she said. Three for the kids, and one for me. She'd never told me what the lizard represented to her before; it seems it represented herself, or her soul. And she wanted to represent us in there as well.

"I'll get a matching tattoo also," I said, without thinking. It just popped out; it seemed right. I've never been one for tattoos. She used to tease me about getting them. Maybe a USB symbol, something really nerdy and funny. But it's never been my thing.

"Really?" she said, incredulous.

"I want to demonstrate my love and devotion." I was still smarting from having let my surgery anxiety put distance between us. And we had just come through that rough period in our marriage, where love really was an action, not merely a feeling. In that moment I wanted desperately to let her know how much I loved her, and forgave her, and wanted her forgiveness, and just... wanted to continue being with her.

It was my last promise.

After she died, it's hard to describe how important keeping that promise became. It sounds macabre, but I had the funeral home take a picture of it for reference. There was a moment of panic when I thought she'd already been cremated. The possible loss of that information—the exact shape and placement of the tattoo—seemed to be a placeholder for everything that had been lost, her memories, her personality, her body. But they got the picture in time. *Something* was preserved.

(It's also hard to describe the extra feeling of loss when she really was cremated. The destruction of her body felt like a one-way door. What did I think was going to happen—that she was going to wake up? And yet it made the loss real, and it hurt like she had died again. I understand now why burial is a custom. You want to leave the door open a crack, even if it doesn't make any sense.)

And so I found myself in a high-end tattoo parlor (the kind with a waiting list), talking about my wife to an ex-con who had turned his life around and loved talking about his wife. The needle hurt like the dickens—your heel right below the ankle is probably not the best place to get your first tattoo—but the pain was something Polly had felt, even if it was long ago, before she met me. I felt like I was experiencing a tiny sliver of her life.

A copy of her gecko tattoo is on my heel now, in the same place. People notice it, and I can tell them the story. I see it every day, and I think about that conversation.

My ring, her ring, her shirt, her tattoo. These are the vestments of my office. Whenever I leave the house I touch her box of ashes, I touch her signature red boots, I touch her glasses, I kiss her ring on its chain. "I carry you with me," I say.

—what makes hope courageous—

you, friend, watched your father collapse in the snow—
and you feel guilty for his death— because you were the
one— who was there— and it doesn't matter if i say you
cannot be guilty— because you know the arguments don't
change the feeling— it is a feeling that needs to be
moved by feelings— you feel inadequate to the task you
felt upon you— (you fear it will happen again)— that
hope was a mistake because it proved mistaken— i have
heard that argument before— hope is often betrayed—
what makes hope courageous is this likelihood— we put
our faith in expertise— would you not have hoped until
the expert declared— he is dead— yet you were not
surprised— you felt betrayed on all fronts— death is a
betrayal of hope— grief, a breathless, hopeless space—

for what was, will never be again– and without breath, or
hope of breath, we gasp goodbye– and it is our gasp–
our transition– our earth inexorably turning away from
the sun– while those around us seem not to notice all
heat, air, hope have instantaneously vanished– abandoned
us– that transition– how can this person cease to exist
when all those i care about suddenly orbit them– "i think
of nothing else, what does it mean to imagine this person
isn't so"– i disagree that death has the power to confer
meaning– to a moment– to an event– even its ability to
confer meaning to life is tenuous and tangential– life
without art is simply a greater horror– but lesser of two
evils does not make meaning– i think life's meaning is
built of meaningful moments– and one's death is the
burden of others– one's own death is the end of steps–
the utter absence of burden– our last emotion, our last
coherent thought is necessarily as random and
insignificant as our first– life is not a fiction and does
not obey its laws– you lost your father and you want to
be sad– instead of panicked– and it feels like it's
just right there– i hope you can sleep tonight– like i
hope that i can– i hope our talking didn't make the
dreams worse– then you've been talking all week– time
has slowed way down– and you feel the break in reality
spreading, gaping– threatening abyss– and wondering if
it will ever beat its right rhythm again– there are drums
in the deep– i wish i could help you from here– i wish i
could help– and i want to say it without bringing the
conversation around to me– perhaps blame is a better

word than guilt- you feel you are to blame for your
dad's death- and that is not the same as the guilt that
comes with grief- it has a different weight- a
different strangle-hold- and you probably should sort
that out- i hope therapy helps- it is hard not to be
impatient with these things- it has already lasted too
long-

Bad Ass Mother

Polly recorded her cover of Leonard Cohen's "Hallelujah" for me when we were dating and trading mixtapes. I have a whole album of her singing. It's like a time capsule of when we were in the Peace Corps together.

It reminds me of when she sang over a campfire at a party in Sagada, Philippines. She always rolled her eyes at the "person at the party with the guitar." But that was her—she was the hot chick at the party with the guitar. And it worked!

So who was this "hard-headed woman"?

She was a "bad ass mother." Polly enjoyed that double meaning. Other people might climb mountains or run marathons, but for Polly, giving birth was her extreme sport. She bore three kids naturally and with no pain relief. She wanted to know if she could do it—if she had the right stuff. Definitely bad ass.

Polly was full of contradictions like that.

She hated running more than anyone, but get her on a hiking trail in the mountains on a nice day, and whoo, there was no stopping her. She'd still be going after everyone else was completely wiped out.

She was a mashup of liberal and traditional. Very much a feminist, she changed her name when we got married and became a homemaker.

She was an atheist. In what may seem a contradiction to some, she was deeply concerned with morality, being a good person, and passing those values along to our children.

Polly could be very shy and slow to make friends, but when she did open up to you, you felt like you had a special relationship with just her. I've heard this over and over in the last few weeks since she died.

She hated bookstores. This woman who read so broadly that she was functionally an English major, hated bookstores. *War and Peace, Moll Flanders, Tom Jones,* everything by Jane Austen—the hard stuff, the rewarding stuff. She told me that she found "18th and 19th century literature to be hilarious in its tediousness." She inhaled books, she loved reading—but don't take her to a bookstore on a date.

She was assiduously honest. Her Peace Corps application form asked whether she'd ever smoked pot— *and Polly said yes.* I don't know about you, but when a government form asks a question like that *you say no.* That answer sent her into a bureaucratic slog that delayed her departure by a year. If she'd lied, we probably would never have met.

She defied the stereotype of the flaky artist—she was no manic pixie dream girl. She was utterly dependable.

Polly distrusted compliments, but she sought out criticism. Or maybe the better word is "critique," in the non-judgmental art-class way.

She had such *confidence*. She knew exactly what she wanted, but she worried about whether what she wanted had value to the wider world.

In the end, Polly was an artist, through and through. She just *couldn't stop making* things. (*Gestures around at the walls*.) Even in the most time-intensive phase of raising small children she couldn't stop, even if it was to do something small like make a T-shirt for Hazel with a warning to others that said "POOR IMPULSE CONTROL."

There's this picture of her with a shirt that says "never trust an artist." She liked to point out that in Plato's *Republic* (which lays out the ideal society), it was only artists who weren't allowed. They're always pushing and questioning and subverting. They even mess with other artists.

Polly was always subverting things in a subtle way. Some assumption you had, some cultural practice we all buy into. But mostly she subverted the mundane.

It could be joyous. Her friend Rachel invited us to this multi-family photo-taking party with a professional photographer. Wine and cheese, everyone dressed up, families with suits and ties and fancy dresses. "We're going as superheroes," she told me. We rolled in there with rubber boots, capes, masks—and our underwear on the outside. It was so embarrassing. It was fantastic. I found out later she didn't even warn Rachel.

Polly told me that a big temptation for the artist (especially performance artists like her) was to force their whole life to be an artwork. And her realization was—who would want to live with someone who would try to do that? But here's the thing—she *kinda did* make her life her art. She couldn't help it. Between injecting color and aesthetics into *everything* (have you seen our house??) and these bursts of magic realism and just *living an authentic life* she really did make her life and our lives into a work of art.

For her MFA show she worked in some performance art by not speaking for several weeks, even outside of the show itself. (As you can imagine, this drove her family nuts.) She hated artist statements—she felt they were pretentiously telling you what to think. At worst they were even wrong about their own art! So, in being silent, she was telling everyone they had to make up their own minds about her show.

She's silent again. Her works of art are here—the pieces on the walls, her children, all of us.

She's silent again. She's not going to tell us what it all means.

She's silent again. But I think we can figure it out.

this dark tower locked- this profound well deepened- empty and yet- suffocating- lost, oh! thomas, lost ridiculousness. of language- wishing for that subtle metaphor to describe- to communicate me- as lost too describe wind through needles of the ponderosa- and the conjured memory of living winter weekends grandparents' study with white snow paper and black handled scissors- why i never know where I remembering always the middle- finding myself always at ends- struck by the ludicrous overstatement- feeling surely clever but fading- like this evening's cotton ball moon hung securely from no doubt, thread- i seek to control its placement in the sky- i seek to control- it's a joke- "i used to be funny," says the little green worm, "i used to have them in stitches"- but i don't know why the fractal flat in the morning- won't dance for me one moment and parades the next- or how that leads me to elevator humming to the elevator music in its head- down the hall and i wishing to be fol as i have been lead- in all seriousness- down the Well- I'm afraid i think I'm dan i suppose i am- sorry- but the words were already half formed when finding i am half healed and half numbstruck half lying in the summer grass- half rainbow vapor half half seeing as I'm yet "it's a curse to be brilliant," you with every and i smile knowing my poetaster still i don't know why i need from you- while nothing i have is good enough, dude- I'm stuck in this half well- half truth- half place- one pulse nearing and sig this dark tower that i am nothing without you- dear old thomas, this dark tower lo this profound well deepened- empty and yet

—sestina—

lit down around the ankles possibly with wings
sailing out on tides of breath exhaled softly from his lips
in the moon glow pale ghost breath as the leaves
turn red by day, grey by night and fall to decay
sometimes i think he doesn't even notice the change
or that i've turned my head to go alone

half the time he's with me he's alone
dreaming in his world of all possible wings
he says there was nothing to start with, so change
is hardly worth discussing as i bite my lips
bearing down on my heels to slow the decay
i batten down the hatches and he leaves

drifting along between his footsteps leaves
finally resting mirroring my futility standing alone
beginning to fret how soon my body will decay
when only yesterday split the cocoon unfurled my wings
began to feel the loneliness of my unkissed lips
pursed and ready anticipating the final change

my eyes to nothing open the single change
took place like first snow falling heavy on the leaves
the limbs bend low as if to touch the lips
of passersby that move down the street alone
to them an afternoon of lover's wings
a chance to forget longing and eventual decay

but upon awakening to night all decay
seems emphasized as inevitable rushing change
all the birds in the world but not enough wings
to escape the turning cycles of time and leaves
fall around him tonight walking home alone
just as they've fallen years before to lips

that could not foresee becoming unrequited lips
or passed over lips losing their curl to decay
and time spent frowning hurt to be left alone
by every prince whose presence promised change
reckoning desperate hope he leaves
you see, by saying i love your formidable wings

i'd sooner deny your lips than clip your wings
be alone eternally than watch your leaves
die fall and decay because i couldn't let you change

Three Haunted Houses

I live down the street from a haunted house. Its roof sags, with holes in it visible from the sidewalk. The back fence leans, where it's not completely fallen down. The grass towers. The windows are boarded up. A piece of paper sticks to the front door that says "CONDEMNED." A truck is parked out front that never moves. The city came in a swarm of vehicles and disconnected the gas and power lines. It's an archetype, like in the movies where kids dare each other to touch the front door or make bets to see who's brave enough to stay overnight.

An old man lives there.

I have to admire his tenacity, but where does he sleep? In the shed? In the basement? Not on the top floor, surely, where the sky is visible and not from a skylight. Are there holes in the floor that he could fall through? Do raccoons live there with him?

The neighborhood rumor is that he lost his partner years ago and he's depressed. In a fit of cleverness and lack of empathy, I started calling him Mr. Havisham. (If you don't remember from high school English class: in *Great Expectations*, Miss Havisham is an old lady who was jilted at the altar years ago. She lives alone in a crumbling house in her threadbare wedding dress, with a rotted wedding cake in the dining room, spider-webs everywhere.)

I understand Mr. Havisham better now. I want to sit there and do nothing, wallowing in the memories, keeping everything frozen and unchanging, while the world moves around me. I think if not for my kids I would join the Havisham club, and let my house crumble and lose my job and be alienated from my family and friends. My kids' needs are manifold and relentless. I must attend to them, or they will make too much noise and interrupt the wallowing.

Mr. Havisham is a warning. His is a possible path that would be all too easy to go down. I have to *get up*. For myself. For my kids. For Polly.

Polly's family mountain cabin was haunted. After three generations of grandmothers and cousins and toddlers and weddings it had accumulated so much memory and nostalgia that even though I was an outsider married in, I could feel it.

The orange shag carpet hadn't changed since the 70s

and the mother of that toddler who just banged his mouth on the coffee table did the same thing to that same coffee table twenty years ago.

The cabin had an elaborate operating procedure, laid down by Grammie in the distant past, and everyone was afraid to violate it. You unlocked these doors, you switched on these switches, you put things back this way. When Polly first brought me there, she sent me down into the sub-basement to turn on the water heater pilot light (which must be turned off when you leave). It was like a dark cave, filled with dust and dead mice. I laid on the ground so I could get a match under the heater, went through a few matches until I got the hang of it, got it lit, scrambled up, and emerged back into the light like Orpheus. Polly nodded, not impressed so much as satisfied, like I'd passed some sort of test.

We went on long hikes in the summer. In the winter we scrounged up old gear from the backs of closets and skied on the river. Kids wandered in the woods and we worried about bears. I joined the family and linked into the chain of emotion and felt the same entitlement to this ancestral homeland in the mountains. Didn't I grow up here, wandering these woods? No, that's Polly's memory.

And then they sold it.

The family got too big, and the voting shares were weird, and the taxes and upkeep were expensive, and they sold it. It was like Charlemagne's heirs splitting up Europe because they couldn't agree. If strict adherence to fairness leads to destruction, what's the point of fairness? I now find myself a big fan of Downton Abbey's "entailment," where the eldest inherits. It's not *fair*, but it preserves the ancestral homeland, which is more important.

For Polly it was like losing her mother all over again. She felt the ghosts in that cabin not just because of the weight of years, but because it was her last link to her mom Nancy, who died when Polly was 18. Can a building have a ghost when it dies?

Nearly a year after Polly's memorial, I went back to the cabin to see what the new owners had done with it. I wanted to walk the nearby open space and put my feet in the river and feel the ghosts, if they were still there. I expected a scrape and a McMansion, but they'd preserved the core original house and only replaced the add-ons. It was surprisingly respectful, for rich out-of-state jackasses.

Risking a trespassing charge, I walked down the gravel driveway and placed my palm against the logs of the original house. The memories are still there, of Grammie and her daughter Nancy Jo and her daughter Polly Jo and our children Peggy Jo and Hazel Maude and Cary Jay. The memories are still there, in the atoms of the wood, even though the windows and the carpet have been replaced. The memories are still there, unchanged, in the trees and the beach by the river and the paths into the mountains.

The cabin isn't dead, though we don't belong there anymore. It's still haunted, even if the new owners can't see the ghosts.

My house is haunted.

When we bought our house as newlyweds, I sat on the steps and looked at its emptiness and thought, "We're going to fill this house with babies." And we did.

Along the way, Polly remade the house. She painted the walls bright colors with "wallpaper" patterns using laser levels or sponges or free-hand. She made valances over the windows, and custom-swagged lamps for the ceiling lights. She had the kids make handprints on sticky paper and pasted it across the stair risers. We hung her art everywhere. She got tired of the kids asking what she was making for dinner and pasted on a kitchen cabinet a quote (in 200pt font) from Gandalf about how much more wonderful the meal will taste if you don't know what it will be.

She remodeled the downstairs bathroom, installing a sliding door and clever shelving and of course painted patterns on the walls. The garage is tricked out with saws and sanders and pegboards. The basement is full of work tables and easels and supplies. She built the kitchen table and the hardwood benches around it. She built Cary's bed out of industrial pipe and made a canopy on top with holes and lights to mimic stars overhead. She repainted my childhood bunkbed (now Peggy and Hazel's) a vivid orange. She built a clever flush-to-the-wall computer table.

There were so many things. I'm sure I've forgotten something. My point is that this house is hers in a visceral way. It's not just that she lived here and her stuff is here. It's that she left her imprint on *everything*. This is the house that Polly built, and we're just living in it.

But that's not the kind of haunting I mean.

In *The Year of Magical Thinking*, Joan Didion describes grief as being crazy, not in the sense of rolling around like a loon, but in the sense of thinking and doing things that don't make sense, like keeping her dead husband's shoes in the closet because he would need them when he came home.

I had a moment—about 48 hours—where I was convinced Polly's ghost was in the house. Doors would be inexplicably open. Things would be moved. The lights in our bedroom wouldn't turn on. There was a strange, burning smell. The whiteboard with her chore list (but not mine) fell off the wall.

Investigating each phenomenon led to something prosaic. The door had a lean I'd never noticed before. The wall plug that the lamps connect to was surprisingly loose and easily bumped. The kids left a punching balloon in the sun. I guess her whiteboard's command strips weren't stuck on as firmly as the others.

I read *Skeptical Inquirer* for fun. I don't go in for actual, literal, non-metaphorical ghosts. And yet this impression of her presence—this cognitive illusion, if you will—just wouldn't go away. I got angry. I spoke to her ashes. "I need something more tangible than pushing shit around. Spell something with pennies. Fold some paper. Do something unambiguous. This house creaking just isn't going to cut it."

The kids and I went on a road trip. When we came back, a not-small part of me expected the house to be a wreck, papers everywhere, tables flipped over, all sorts of unexplainable commotion. She'd had a whole week after all. Even attenuated ghost strength should be able to do something in a week.

The house was as we left it.

In one sense, the illusion faded. But in another, it's still there. I still talk to her, out loud, with my voice. My heart is convinced that we will meet again someday. (And I'm still not sure about that whiteboard.) When I read to the kids at night, we lie in a pile on our bed—in the room where Polly died—and I wonder if she can hear us. Can she hear our laughter when I do a funny voice, or deliver the book's joke well? Can she hear me when I talk to her ashes?

This desire to *believe that they're okay* is so strong, it warps our minds. It's the literal craziness of grief. It's the magical thinking that somehow, *somehow*, she's out there waiting for me. It's a form of denial, these beliefs in the afterlife and ghosts and visitations. The truth is too hard to bear, so our minds form these illusions. They're very convincing. At this point I just throw up my hands and accept the cognitive dissonance.

I'm more sympathetic to these beliefs now, even if I don't share them. I used to think they came from a narcissistic fear of our own deaths. But I've changed. Now I know that they come from this bottomless pain of loss— the horror of the end of someone you love.

I don't mind being wrong. Everyone wants atheists to be wrong. It's ok. I just want Polly to be able to hear me when I tell her how much I miss her.

—cabin fever—

You do not belong here.
You will never belong here.
This piece of sky, this bit of ground.
These walls, this roof, this temple, sanctuary, cemetery.

You beg a souvenir, a proof, but its life extinguishes as
you walk away. You only have ashes, the fleeting ashes.

You don the cloak of ignorance to shield you from the
icy pain. You seek to sever the concepts from the fact,
but you cannot escape knowing. You know, you know, the
fact held the power, the significance. You know the
memories will not suffice to stem the grief.

You want the shadows here to scream, slam doors, storm
off. They just stand with you echoing your impotence,

waiting to disappear. These shadow ghosts, old holes from old griefs, they resided here. They go to nowhere. The father, the mother, yourself. Lost. You cannot take them with you for they are this place. And this place no longer exists.

You do not belong here. You will never belong here, again.

You take stock of the hits, the balm refuses to coalesce.

there's a folded up piece of paper i've been keeping pressed in this book- each time i open the book to write- the paper falls out- the paper contains what i wrote the weekend i said goodbye to the cooper cabin- so, its appearance is loaded- and i don't want to read it- the paper is clearly a metaphor- yet i know that reading it won't actually change things- i could let/make myself read it every day- and it wouldn't be this cathartic thing- a healing thing- i don't want to heal- i don't want to obsessively pick at the wound either- and so i don't lose the piece of paper and i don't read the piece of paper- and i contemplate that- the stupid dance-the cabin- a fairy world- must be left as if no human had been there- must be entered and exited through a grimy, disturbing underworld- you must remember the special dance that brings the fairy world to life- you must repeat it backwards when you leave or it might be destroyed-

the cabin- feeble star- ever since i can remember- the essence that might be snatched away from us at any turn- the potential development- the encroaching dump- the poison river- our own failure to preserve- the loss that will be the loss of all losses-

i am sick when i think about the fate of the cabin- i try to dodge the feeling of inevitable loss- to imagine the future where it lives in perfect perpetuity- forever a warm hearth and hearty laughter to receive me-

the cabin- is such an indelible part of my identity- would i continue to be myself without it?- would i finally be myself without it?

Parting Pro

Parting Pro Login
Your death notification is complete
I can't imagine
Three kids?
My condolences
Thinking of you
And the grief that you must deal with
polly@mail.com, you have no events scheduled today
On behalf of the bank and myself
The inheritance process begins
We're sorry for your loss
If there's anything I can do
Sent you a $100 e-gift card from Grubhub
Thinking of you and your family
This is your wife? Beautiful…
You should come visit us

Welcome back
How are you?
There are no words
There are no words

—something helpful—

i am still unsure what to write— i would like to say
something helpful— but, perhaps, i won't be that person
in her life— you are a smart, independent, beautiful
woman— mysterious, too— that comes with the
introversion— there will be those that find it intriguing
and those that are turned away by it— and those happy
few who don't seem to notice it at all and become your
true friends— what advice shall i give you?— what can i
say that you might find helpful— today, some day?— i
don't know what problems you face— only the problems i
have faced— sexiness is an internal quality— some will
see it and some won't— i made the mistake of believing
school-time was a practice life— that real life— the
real world— was waiting beyond that— and so i thought
the choices i made there didn't count— but it turns out
there is only real life— you have been in the real world

since you were conceived– and the choices you make
now, the thoughts and opinions you have today are
important and valid– and they will affect your future–
they do affect the people around you– i don't mean to
frighten you– or imply that there's some way to know if
you're making good choices– the right choices– or
forming the right thoughts and opinions– but just be
aware that you are important– and you are just beginning
to learn to take care of yourself– this is the most
important job we have in life– as we can only, truly take
care of ourselves– and we are the only ones we can take
care of– it's very hard work– it means being honest with
ourselves about who we are, what we want, what we need–
about who we surround ourselves with– what we choose to
do– it means keeping ourselves healthy physically,
emotionally and spiritually– when we are sick, it means
giving ourselves time and permission to heal– when we
are well, it means continuing to do the same boring things
over and over and over– like brushing your teeth,
exercising, doing laundry– it means, recognizing when
you're beating yourself up excessively– and stopping–
it means, remembering that you are smart, beautiful,
strong without needing someone else to tell you– these
may seem like simple things to do– but they aren't– life
is hard work– even when you enjoy what you're doing–

Sometimes A Man Is an Island

I live on an island. It's more of an atoll, really, or a sturdy sandbar.

Sometimes tidal waves sweep over it, and I swirl around, drowning, grasping for the ground.

Sometimes the tide simply comes up fast. There is little warning to get to high ground.

Sometimes the tide stays up. I try to float for as long as I can, or stand vertically and bob, taking a breath whenever my head comes up.

Sometimes the tide stays low. I build a little lean-to out of driftwood, where the kids and I can live. Did I mention I have children on this island? What kind of a parent would bring children to a place like this?

Sometimes the tide disappears entirely. There are miles and miles of sand, an endless desert, and I choke on the dust. I find puddles and thrust my face into them, trying to drown. Have you ever tried to drown in half an inch of water? It's supposed to be easy, but it isn't.

Sometimes the island (atoll) is a narrow strip surrounded by water. There isn't much room, and you have to be careful not to fall in, but you can do it if you're careful.

Sometimes planes soar overhead, dropping supply crates. Sometimes the tide sweeps the crates away, and other times they smash to pieces. But occasionally, they land intact and I can unpack them.

Sometimes I get a message in a bottle. Sometimes one of the crates has pen and paper, and I can send reply bottles.

Sometimes the kids and I stare across the expanse of water, and wonder if one day when the tide goes out it will expose a land bridge. Or maybe there will be a boat. Or maybe we could make a raft out of the crates and driftwood.

Sometimes it's even cozy, when the tide isn't too high, and we can sit in the lean-to and have a fire. It can even feel safe on this island.

Sometimes.

—line dancing—

a bleeding sun set tonight— on practice for a dance that
originated on the other side of the world— i'm learning
my own cultural practices from a bunch of small town
islanders— and i'm the one with cowboy boots— they tell
me i'm shaking it wrong— and i tell them i know how to
shake it for real— still, it's fun to learn a line dance—
never been one for country music— though i got
extremely drunk at a country music bar once— after
throwing myself at the guitarist in the band much to the
amusement and encouragement of his band members—
ending our brief encounter by intimating that i don't
like country music— unable to imagine that any sane
person would— lesson learned— i concluded the night
making out with an overweight trucker with white hair—
so, yes, i'm afraid i know how to shake it— and i also
know that what's fun about line dancing is the bravado,

little improvisations, and the ultimate sexiness of tight
jeans and cowboy boots- and it's painful to me to watch
these women turn line dancing into the stiffest, most
unimaginative activity possible- i want to tell them, "the
fun is making it sexy!"- but i refrain not wanting to
explain that sexy doesn't really mean pretty, or comely-
is not really appropriate for children- and it
embarrasses me when they tell me i am- because i didn't
join the Peace Corps to be found sexy by middle aged
school teachers- but if i'm going to have to line dance-
then you better believe i'm going to be sexy-

Trigger Finger

I'm falling into the black...

It's 2023, the first summer after my wife Polly died, and I'm on a lake in Arkansas teaching our three kids how to water-ski. My first time on skis in twenty years *but I've still got it.* The second time up, I pass the critical moment where it's easiest to fall and am about to skim along the surface. Then a CRACK like an explosion, and I'm in the water, my hands on fire. I lie back and let the life vest hold me as the boat zooms off. I'm cursing like a dad whose kids are out of earshot. *What just happened?* The best I can reconstruct it: the tow rope snapped just inches from the hand-hold. Like those horror stories about tug-o-war, the energy released through the line and it whip-cracked across my fingers.

It feels like I have the mother of all finger jams, but

the x-ray shows otherwise. The little bone that formed the tip of my right index finger had a piece snapped off, floating above the joint. It's called a "mallet finger," which sounds like a joke, or a grunge band. No amount of splinting or casting can fix something like this. It's going to require surgery. It's going to require Going Under.

I'm falling into the black...

I stared at the liability release form, all the things that can go wrong. BLOOD CLOTS loomed like it had a spotlight on it, or like it was written in a different font. Blood clots are a standard risk of surgery. Everyone knows this. What is the likelihood of a *fatal* blood clot? It is very low. so low that everyone focuses on the general anesthesia, which is itself very low risk. And yet.

And yet, that's how Polly died. A "very large" blood clot, said the autopsy, right at the saddle where the lung arteries join together. "Natural causes," said the autopsy, a week into recovery from straightforward outpatient surgery. A known risk of abdominal work, higher than other kinds, but still very low risk. And yet. How do I understand risk now? Do I have the right to put myself at risk like this? Am I also going to be taken from my kids? When I schedule this surgery, am I scheduling the date of my own death, like Polly did?

I'm falling into the black...

I'm overreacting, aren't I? It's just a stupid finger, a straightforward outpatient surgery—how dangerous could it be? But there was that widow I ran into at the kids' grief camp, the one whose husband died of the same thing: a blood clot after routine ankle surgery. I'm now a connoisseur of the improbable. Maybe I can just…*skip it?* Yep, kids, your dad spent the rest of his life living in fear, never taking any risks. And here's the janky, broken forefinger to prove it. What a role model!

This "trigger finger" needs a trigger warning. It's dredging up PTSD thoughts. It rhymes so much with Polly's surgery—it's routine, it's easy, nothing could go wrong. The hardest thing was telling the kids—I don't want them to worry about losing another parent.

I'm falling into the black…

They wheel me into the O.R., which is like watching a movie where they put the camera on the gurney and roll it down the hallway. I'm sobbing; I'm grieving; I'm terrified; it's too much. They strap my arm down. They put the gas mask over my face. They tell me to start counting. I'm staring at the lights on the ceiling. And then…

I am in the black…

Is Polly down here? Will I have a vision of her? I want to see her, and have her tell me it's ok. I want her to forgive me for being a mediocre husband, and I want her to be proud of me, to tell me I'm raising the kids like she would. I want her to apologize for leaving us, and I want to forgive her. I want her to hold out her hands and ask me to come with her. I want to go with her, singing that Death Cab For Cutie song we used to sing to each other, where the singer melodramatically promises to follow his lover into the black.

But can I leave my children? I've made this choice between wife and kids before. When our daughter Hazel was born she came out purple, and *stayed* purple. The doctors clustered around her and I held her tiny hand thinking she would die. In the chaos, they began wheeling Polly away, her afterbirth gone wrong again. She had to go into surgery or she would bleed to death; she might not come back. They started wheeling Hazel away in the opposite direction to the NICU, with her crowd of doctors. I was being towed along by her purple hand. *Who do I go with?* I made fleeting eye contact with my wife. I went with our child.

I am in the black...

My phone lay on the ground and the tinny voice of the 911 dispatcher talked me through CPR. I breathed into Polly's mouth and her chest *rose*, but her motion had its origin in me, not her. The paramedics burst through the front door, terrifying the kids, who had innocently been eating breakfast downstairs. The paramedics took over. I stood up, watching them go to work. They had to have known she was gone—I knew she was gone—but they went to work anyway. Even the smallest chance that there was still life in there was worth this grotesque playacting. One of them told me I could stay and watch while they did this. I saw her there, lying on the floor, and wanted to stay with her and hold her cold hand and hope. But the kids were downstairs, lost among strangers. I stood up straight and I looked at my wife for the last time, and I said, "I need to be with my children."

I am in the black…

If Polly is down here, I can't see her. How can I go with her? Could I look her in the eye, and say that yes I also left our children behind? I abandoned them to be with you. She would never accept me, if this is how I got there. I'm surprised she's not going to follow me back out! How does Heaven contain all the mothers who were taken from their children?

I can't go with Polly. I have to go back. And not just because that's what she would want. I have to stay for *them*. They can't lose both parents. They have to grow up to be non-broken adults, and I'm the only one who can see to it. This is the vow I didn't know I was making, when we had kids. It transcends marriage vows, and we didn't even need to say any words. I just had to see these babies come out of my wife, and hold them, and cry with joy together over these beautiful, loud, slimy messes.

The vow is that I would leave Polly behind to save our children. The wagon train of our life will roll on. We can stop to bury her on the side of the trail, but we can't stay. There's not enough food, and the kids don't know how to drive a wagon, or which way to go, and winter is bearing down.

I am rising from the black…

It's 2024, the second summer after my wife Polly died, and I'm on a lake in Iowa teaching our three kids how to water-ski. My first time on skis in a year, but my finger is healed and I'm able to grip the bar—I pull up easily and skim across the water. I can see my kids waving to me from the back of the boat. The rope does not snap. A blood clot did not kill me. They can see me grinning. I'm trying to show them that—*somehow*—we can still live, though most of the time *they're* showing *me*. Who is pulling who? The wind blows across my face. The sun shines down.

I am rising from the black...

—birth question—

i wake up to doubt— and so early— and so hungry— i'm not
sure how long i'll be able to focus past it— what is my
birth question?— will i be strong enough to get through it
naturally?— will it go smoothly?— will i be able to
confront my fears in time for the birth?— will i be a
consistent mother?— will i have the energy to do all
this?— will i rise to meet our needs or will i neglect
something of vital importance?— will i be capable and
willing to self-sacrifice or will my selfish nature
prevail?— will i get enough sleep?— will we start
fighting all the time?— will i enjoy sex ever again?—
will i be a good wife/mother/homemaker?— will i have
the energy to work on projects?— will i have time to
myself?— will i become more flexible?— or respond by
becoming more inflexible?— will i be faced with my own
death in birth?— will it sear me?— will i be faced with

the death of my baby in birth?- will i be able to "share"
this experience with aaron- or even the millions of
women who've given birth?- will this birth be joyous, or
terrifying, or tragic?- or a combination too complex to
describe?- or will it be mundane?- will i feel trapped
by this new responsibility?- or invigorated by it?- will i
change?- what if i don't?- will i be utterly unprepared
for birth no matter what i do?- will the first signs of
labor be exciting or terrifying?- what will i regret not
doing?- what am i denying the reality of?- i am
overwhelmed by all the "stuff"- and all the possible
paths we might take to get where we're going- i am
afraid that i will cause this baby to perish by lying the
wrong way- by eating the wrong things- by forgetting to
take care of her- or refusing to- i am overwhelmed by
all the various voices that seem to be asking me to be
something other than myself- as though the changes i am
already experiencing aren't enough- i'm afraid i'll be
jealous of your relationship with our child- i'm afraid
i'll resent the time and affection you'll give to her- i'm
afraid i won't have the energy to give you the time and
affection you need- will i have emotional control when i
give birth?- will i want to be alone?- or afraid to be
alone?- will i be both and piss you off with my
contradictions?- will i hurt your feelings?- will i be a
model mother in some respect?- how will i succeed?-
how will i fail?- will i be able to accept my failures
and move on?- will i be able to feel proud of my
successes?- will i totally give up on my dream of being

an artist?— will being a mother inspire me to be my best self?— will i continue with the same old struggles as before?— or will they subtly change?— will i ever contribute meaningfully to a community?— or will my children become my contribution?— will i easily navigate the pitfalls of modern medicine?— have i already doomed myself by not being able to think all the way to the birth when we started— or, indeed, until just recently?— will i have charming and graceful children?— will choosing family names pass on the tragic flaws of those who owned the names previously?— or serve to connect my children to those who've gone before them?— will my giving birth scare or disgust you?— will you be there without judgment?— will you be confident?— will i find confidence?— will i cry?— will i be vulnerable?— will i be willing to see people afterwards?— will my body ever be elegant again?— will i feel special as a mother?— or ordinary?— will i have the courage to ask my questions at our appointment today?— i was full of conviction yesterday but woke up full of doubts today—

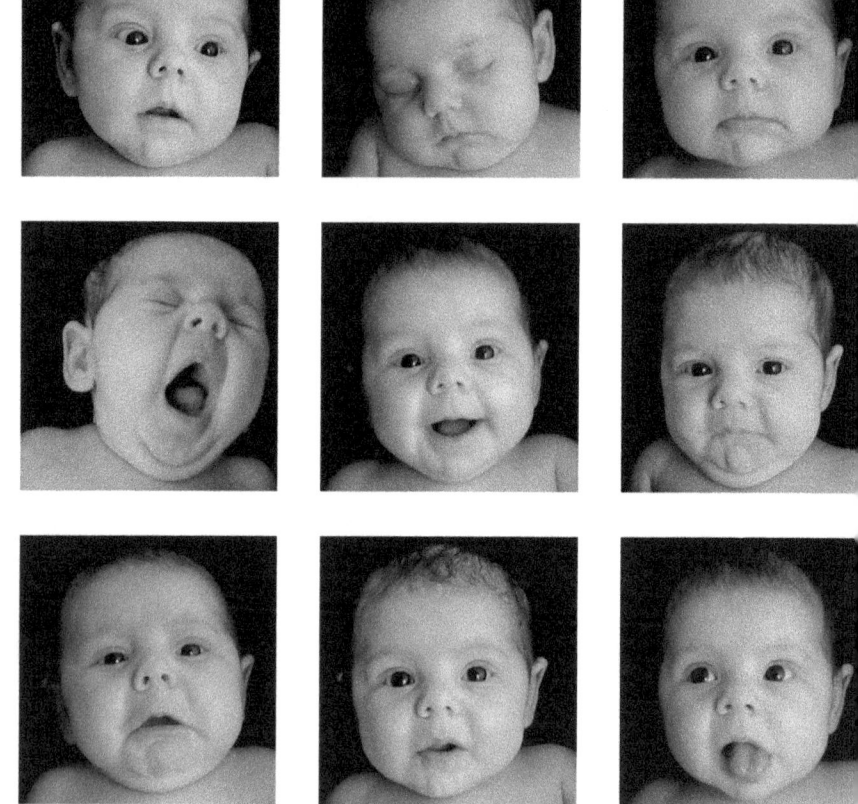

Soledad

That morning the lion emerged from his lair, face covered in blood. The hood was up on his full-suit pajamas, the furry mane around his head, the ears peeking out the top. His tail swished behind him as he walked. Was he a were-lion, the suit transforming him by night into a beast on the prowl? Had he snuck out the window in the wee hours and mauled a deer?

Sadly no, it was a bit more prosaic: Cary (7) had a nose bleed in the night and had slept right through it. His pillow looked like a crime scene. His nose and cheek were a crusty red-brown smear.

My kids have all had their share of Dramatic Health Freakouts, but Cary has had some doozies.

There was the time he opened the door into his toe and ripped the nail clean off. There was a lot of blood from that one!

There was the time around Polly's memorial when Cary began to complain of itching and burning from his rear end. It turned out he had impetigo, a huge red rash. It must have taken some time to get that big but I hadn't been in the habit of seeing his butt regularly since he was potty trained. It felt like a sign from the Mother's Chorus—*you can't do this, solo dad. This is beyond you.* A mother would have known this was coming; she would somehow have worked in a glance at her naked kids' butts just to make sure nothing was wrong. Well, I got a good look at his rear for the next six weeks, as I applied the scifi-named "mupirocin" antibiotic twice a day. ("It's time for your mupi," we'd joke.)

Physical health is easy, though, compared to mental health, discipline, and Raising Your Kids Right. That's where I really hear the Mother's Chorus.

One night when it was time to get ready for bed, Cary rushed to the bathroom ahead of his sisters so he could beat them to brushing his teeth. (I was always on him for getting ready for bed... super... slowly..., and lately he'd been overcompensating.) His sister needed something out of the bathroom, but he thought she was trying to sneak in ahead of him. He slammed the sliding door into her, which hurt, and kicked her out.

That kind of thing makes me crazy, so I forced open the sliding door and told him he needed to go to his room. He got really upset, defending his turf. I was mad because it's a particular button with me when the kids are violent with each other, especially boy-on-girl. He was yelling; I was trying not to yell. It started escalating.

Here's the thing about Cary's psychology: you can't

win by escalating. With the girls, they'll back down, but Cary is like The Hulk—anger only makes him stronger. If you bring a gun to Cary's knife fight, he whips out a machine gun; you counter with a bazooka, he sees your bazooka and raises an ICBM. It doesn't go well after that.

It got to the point that I was considering wrestling him out of that narrow bathroom door, but I was afraid I'd hurt him. Cary is quite strong, and the grip I'd have to use would probably hurt. Maybe if I suddenly yelled real loud it would snap him out of it like a dash of water, and then he could go to his room and cool things down.

I'm describing this like I was detached and rational, solving the argument like a puzzle. I wasn't being rational—I was rationalizing. I was angry. I yelled at him, "GO TO YOUR ROOM." It seemed like a good idea at the time.

For what it's worth, it worked. He stomped up to his room. I'd seen his ICBM and raised him a Death Star. Boom!

I sat there in the bathroom, the anger draining away, listening to my son cry in his room. I could hear the Mother's Chorus, all in unison: *this isn't how you do it*. But more importantly, this isn't how *Polly* would do it. She'd had this same escalation problem with Cary—the usual tools weren't working. She read up on some child psychology to get new tools, she tried new things.

And ultimately she was *creative* as a parent. When I describe her creativity to people, they brush it off. "Sure, she was an artist, of course she was creative." I think it's more impressive than that. Creativity across domains is very rare. For example, I'm pretty creative with computers but outside of that area… not so much. But I was going to have to learn.

Not for the last time, I asked myself, *What would Polly do?*

I went up to Cary's room and sat on the bed. I didn't say anything. He huffed and turned away from me. I stared at the clock for a full five minutes, just letting it be quiet. I picked up a book, *Robert The Rose Horse*, that I knew he liked. It was the book that finally got him interested in reading, back when he was little, when I would read Robert's explosive sneezes with as much volume and noise as I could muster.

I started reading it. Cary opened one eye.

"And Robert got that f-f-f-f-funny f-f-f-feeling…," I read. Cary turned toward me.

By the second gigantic sneeze, he'd snuggled up to me so he could see the pictures.

Later, I talked to him about what had happened. Slamming the door on his sister wasn't ok, but neither was letting it get out of hand like I had. We said sorry to each other. We were ok.

The Mother's Chorus nodded in approval: *adequate. We'll see how you do on the next one.*

"Dad!!!" read the chat with a video invite, "Dad join pls." It was ten minutes old.

My oldest kid and I were coming out of her therapy session when I saw the messages. The waiting room is a very effective Faraday Cage—I can't get cell service in there, and their wi-fi is spotty. And after several uneventful months of letting the other kids hang out at home while going to therapy for my oldest, I had gotten out of the habit of checking my phone every five minutes.

Hazel (10) had offered to cook dinner that night. Normally I rush to cook dinner early before evening therapy, but that day was kind of crazy and I ran out of time. But Hazel stepped in and said she could grill the burgers and we'd all eat together when we got home. She'd used the grill before, and it's not like burgers are particularly complicated. Also—and this is the thing that will really trip you up—Hazel is very competent, and *very* convincing. Even the Mother's Chorus would find it easy to forget she's just a child.

She had turned the gas on, but forgotten to push the igniter. After letting it warm up for five minutes, she came back to put the burgers on, but it wasn't hot. "That's odd," she thought, opening up the lid.

Then she pushed the igniter button.

The propane gas, which had been quietly collecting in the bottom of the grill, erupted into a ball of fire—shooting into the air, sweeping across Hazel's face. She fell back, shaken. She tried to call me. No answer. She tried to chat me. No answer. She tried to video call me. No answer.

As soon as I saw her message, I called her from the car. I'm not sure how much time had passed by this point. Ten minutes? As she told me the story, I began driving faster and faster. I tore into the neighborhood with images of my precious daughter's face horribly disfigured, streaks of third degree burns, blackened crisps of skin. In my mind she looked like Khan at the end of *Star Trek II*.

Just like a dad to be so cavalier about danger, says the Mother's Chorus. *We've got Child Protective Services on speed-dial.*

I got home and hugged her. Hazel looked like a normal kid, if a little shaken up, though she smelled of burning hair. Her face was covered with tiny little ashes, wisps from her bangs burned into black flakes. We talked through what had happened, and I explained her mistake and why the grill acted like it did. She was lucky she'd opened the lid first, which gave the gas a few seconds to disperse.

I had her take a shower so that she could re-center herself, but I had an unspoken motive. I had heard of people burning their eyebrows off. Maybe her eyebrows were just ashes, sitting there on her skin waiting to fall away. I paced in the hallway and talked to her through the door.

When she got out, her face was clear. She was fine. I laughed with relief and hugged her again. There was just the littlest stub of hair where her bangs had been. In the coming weeks they slowly grew out, annoyingly shorter than the rest of her hair; they bothered her. I called them her "fire bangs."

Hazel still helps out with the cooking now and then. But nobody uses that grill unless I'm around.

───────

Peggy (12) came up to me, holding out her underwear and shoving them at me, demanding, "What is *this?*" There was a small diluted red-turning-brown smear. "Well, I guess it's finally happening," I said. I think Peggy knew the answer, but she had just wanted me to say it. She rolled her eyes and groaned, like here's some new chore she has to deal with. "But it's also exciting, isn't it?" I said, and I think she's starting to come around.

Oh, no, says the Mother's Chorus, *a dad talking about his daughter's period. This should be good.*

It's gotten heavier day by day. Peggy wanted to go swimming, so we sat in the bathroom and she tried to put in a tampon. (Fortunately, we have a kit of various sizes that a mom-friend gave her.) I held up the frank illustrations from *The Care And Keeping of You*, and we both laughed nervously. My other daughter hovered around the edges, concerned, trying to be supportive. My son was downstairs, oblivious. Surprisingly, my mom (who happened to be in town) wasn't invited in.

I thought her impulse to go swimming was going to outweigh the weirdness of a tampon, but ultimately it was just too strange yet and she ended up not doing it. We have a ton of tampons, so what if we throw away a few figuring this out?

I thought for sure when this moment came and there was literally any other woman around that Peggy would pick them instead of her awkward dad who didn't even know that tampons can have "applicators." But she chose me, and we bumbled through it, and I think we did ok.

I wish Polly were here for this. Not to spare me the awkwardness, but just so she could see that her daughter is growing up. I don't know what she planned to commemorate this moment, or what her own mother did.

But I bet she was planning *something*. She was too intentional to just let this sort of thing pass by.

Polly had a tradition where right at the end of a pregnancy we'd go to the Dushanbe Tea House and have a tea ceremony to welcome the change into our lives. We even had one right before the surgery that ended her life.

So I adapted Polly's idea and took Peggy to the Tea House, and we drank a pot of tea and talked about growing up and welcomed the change into our lives. I don't know if that's what Polly would have done, but it was "on brand," you might say. It's something she *could* have done.

Months later, I found a letter that Polly had written her oldest niece years ago:

dear kenya,

congratulations on getting your period— i am so excited that you have crossed this important threshold into womanhood!— maybe it seems like a funny thing to find exciting, but having a period really is cool— yes, it can be inconvenient and even embarrassing at times— it can also be a relief, a joy, a disappointment— it's kind of magical to have this cyclic thing in our lives that can represent so many different emotions— as you get older, you may find that your period gains meaning— it becomes a regular reminder of the depth of your experiences.

it seems many women get kind of stuck on the
"inconvenience" of it— but it's so much more
rewarding to recognize that a period is a sign
of health and the ability to create life—
having just crossed that next threshold into
womanhood myself, i can tell you the
"inconvenience" is well worth the trouble

love,
aunt polly

I printed a copy for Peggy, to show what her mom would have said to her. We were on the right track after all! She taped it to the inside of her art journal, but modified with "dear ~~kenya~~ peggy," and "love, ~~aunt polly~~ mom."

Now I get monthly(ish) reports on when Peggy's period is starting, when it's done, how heavy it is, bloating, cramps—all the stats. I don't ask for it, but Peggy wants to share it with *someone*, and the someone she wants to share it with is her dad.

I've read about the endless judgement that mothers feel. Society puts so much expectation on them. Men and children (assuming there's a difference) demand so much. Moms expect so much from themselves. It's like there's a Greek chorus in the back of every mother's mind, telling them what they're doing wrong, how they're not measuring up. They try to tamp it down, rationalize it away, not listen to it. But the Mother's Chorus is always there.

There is no Father's Chorus. Male inadequacy runs along a different axis. Society just figures if you're keeping the kids alive, you've done more than enough. It's a pleasant shock to find a dad aiming for a higher bar. Though the compliment can be worse than an insult, like saying, "you're pretty smart, for a woman," but for men.

Something happened to me, because I started hearing the Mother's Chorus. *You're a pretty good parent*, they say, *for a dad*. They'll never be satisfied.

There's a terrible loneliness to the solo parent—the *soledad* of the sole dad. But I can feel myself hooked into the lineage of mothers, going all the way back. I can hear Polly's voice in it. I can hear my own mother's, who raised my sister and me as a single parent. I can do this. All I ask from the Chorus is: don't judge me like a dad, with its insultingly low bar.

If I have to be judged, judge me like I'm a *mom*.

—i wondered how i could love you—

-peggy-

she is five weeks old— we are still getting used to her existence— i find it equally challenging to fit in all the "for five minutes" activities i'm supposed to do with her as i did with the dog— i was surprised to discover that i physically needed to hold her— still need to hold her but the chemical dependency is lessened— i thought i would want to hold her— like a new toy i wanted to learn— but that's the intellectualization of a deeper need— our logic says why do we need to dominate this thing— but when we are away from it for too long we start to hit the rocky shoals— we start to sink— so, for that first month or so, it isn't really a help to have someone else hold the baby for more than fifteen or twenty

minutes- or to take the baby so you can sleep- you can
sleep when the baby sleeps- but sleep with the baby-

-hazel-

the morning of your birth- the false sun shone through
the endless night- and you held your breath- as we
pushed you into the world- you were strong and well-
and purple and blue- so mightily you waited for the
air- i slept in the crevices to build the strength i
needed to bring you to the light- your father was wild
with excitement- holding me- supporting us- as we
worked together to birth you- and when you came he
cried with joy- and i held you close- so close-

-cary-

i was a mother to two daughters when i answered the
phone- standing in a parking lot i learned you were a
boy- and i wondered how i could love you- the plans i
had for three girls dashed- and i worried for seven
months how would i love you- after a night of pain- we
sent for your grandparents to care for your sisters- at
the hospital you were born and i looked upon your face
for the first time and thought, "oh, i love you."-

the minotaur – the passion force – in my time – it ___ ___ my clothes – slipping in
water faster than i can hold on and maybe ___ ___ maybe the search for th
that has no key and i'll do it – i'll ___ ch – listen ___ suck as my hands clo
down – as my mind shrivels up ___ the power rushes from my body – gone
the freedom of having no resp___ ___ ity is mine to gamble nothing within i'll sett
back into the life unbou___ unbound by the possibility of infinity but
do it – i won't close that do___ because i have a feeling – ode to feelings – m
i be led astray but might ___ ___ into a world of moons and endlessness – th
___ something everything me___ ___ then me or you or the combination there
___ this darkness – the powe___ ___ this – the life here in exists – ___ ___ beyo
what – oh this, because th___ rather insignificant – but let the minotaur
my child – don't abort this ___ ___ allow the change. allow the ___ allow th
self possession that comes from ___ knowing ___ does come next ___ but may
onight knocking on the door ___ all in – seize upon raindrops coming through
the hair of the stranger standi___ next to me – hold my ___ – it's simple
infinity is simple – death is simple ___ the minotaur ___ simple – love is
anything but – just look at me – as ___ ___ you ___ don't know you at
i'm willing to bet there's a potent___ minotaur within your ovaries – sh
shaken shook real hard want me to give up on me and life – to say f
you too – ang___ ___ is brothers to passion – i held it to my breast – wishing i
describe the moon setting fearful in the sky like it has goodbyes as
as i do – but there's peace holding this with the moon and words are but
meant to capture your fanc___ all full joy and jubilation – i could escape fro
being shoved into the stream with all the other fish – i look back an
like my minotaur – my passion ___ my reason reasonless and failing to g
up in the morning – all becau___ i've lost – i know that life is a thi
i'll get it back – i'll get revenge ___ got my monsters in bed with me –
in my minotaur – i've got infin___ and chaos and simple simple. sim
___ the full me ___ is with me ___ with every beat – every ounce of
extract see ___ a chance ___
___ taur –

The Widow-er!

In *What Doesn't Kill Us: The New Psychology of Posttraumatic Growth*, Stephen Joseph opens with:

> As a child of the 1960s and 1970s I loved American comic books. … Spiderman [sic] was my favorite of all. Physically transformed after a bite from a radioactive spider, he finds himself gifted with strange superpowers. But that is not what made him my favorite. It isn't until after his Uncle Ben dies at the hands of a criminal that Peter Parker realizes his calling in life, turning his newfound powers to fighting crime. […] Stories about superheroes are metaphors for the challenges we face in life. […] Ordinary people have the power to live lives just as

> dramatic and driven as those of superheroes,
> overcoming traumas no less daunting.

Sounds appealing, doesn't it? Especially to someone like me, who has pulp superheroes infused in my psyche.

But this is garbage.

It tracks one of the great pulp tropes—The Bad Ass Forged By Tough Living. Perhaps its purest expression is in *Dune*, where the Sardaukar of the hellish Salusa Secondus are defeated by the Fremen of the even *more* hellish Arrakis (with a little help from Bene Gesserit martial arts). Later in the series, after Arrakis is remade into a watery paradise, the Fremen become weak and long for the days when they were awesome.

The trope shows up everywhere, and is deeply embedded in heroic genre fiction. It's a Compensating Factor—the audience will identify more with the hero if in exchange for his powers he had to suffer, and (even better) if he has to continue to suffer. (This is one of the challenges of writing great Superman stories. Despite his Moses-like tragic origin story and the constant burden of saving everyone, he doesn't really have a Compensating Factor.)

Life is not like this. Your character sheet doesn't have the same number of "character points" as everyone else, where you choose to put points into Tragic Backstory and get Cool Superpower.

Yes, people bounce back from trauma and loss and it is important to say so. From the outside it can seem shocking. "I can't imagine what you're going through" is often said because our imagination overdoes it. Surely you must be rolling around on the ground 24/7, pulling your hair out, sobbing uncontrollably for days at a time.

On the day my wife died, I watched the social workers take my kids outside and play games with them, and my kids were eager to do so. You can only sit around stunned for so long before you have to move. Eventually you have to eat. This permission slip needs signing. That backyard dog shit isn't going to pick itself up. Holding grief in your mind for long periods (like holding any thought) becomes repetitive and boring. Your mind wanders. The little things you have to do build up and build up, until you're walking around talking and greeting people like a normal human person.

I've learned to cook. I was never very good at it, and my wife was *very* good at it. (Trope alert: Man Learns To Cook After Wife Dies—film at eleven.) It was important to me to be able to cook the things she cooked, especially her and the kids' favorites, because the sense memory of those meals keeps her alive in our hearts. There's also something about standing where she stood, holding the pans she held, trying to remember how she made a dish, that blurs the ego boundaries, and makes me feel not just connected with her but that I *am* her, that she's within me.

Is cooking a superpower that I've gained in exchange for my dead wife?

The thing to remember is this—whatever you gain in "posttraumatic growth" is dwarfed in comparison to the loss. Cooking Skill may be worth 100 character points, but Loss Of Wife costs 1 million points. You are not coming out ahead. There is no Compensating Factor.

The trouble with framing it this way is that this mode

of thinking exists on a spectrum, and it's very easy to slide on into the next logical step—that it is *good* she died because now I'm awesome. If we take this assertion literally—that trauma is a crucible in which to make superheroes—then why don't we do it on purpose?

MARVEL COMICS GROUP PRESENTS

First Sensational Issue!

After his wife was taken from him by the **forces of nature**, Aaron Simmons realized that he had become **awesome** and understood in a **flash of insight** his calling—to make more **awesome people**! In particular, **women,** because he had absorbed so much **feminism** from his **late wife**!

Now he roams the countryside in a **neverending quest** to make **women awesome** by taking their **husbands** from them in tragic "accidents!"

He has become—**The Widow-er**!

This is obviously horrifying (and not just because of the pun). Of course, this exact reasoning is what we attribute to God, who would Know which husbands to kill for maximum effectiveness.

Is a Widow-er God more justified than a human one? In the famous *When Bad Things Happen to Good People,* Harold Kushner pulls the rug out from under the ways we justify and excuse God for the terrible events visited upon us, imagining those words as applied to famous despots and criminals. Surely Stalin has a Plan, which we may not understand, but in the fullness of time will reveal itself to have been wonderful and good? Does it make sense to use those words for God? Why do we call evil, when it is done by the Creator, good?

In marveling at the ability of people to pick up the pieces after trauma, we become overexcited and get things exactly backwards. Just because we can make lemonade out of lemons doesn't mean we should *celebrate* lemons, or infer that lemons are made deliberately for the purpose of making lemonade.

What, then, is the *point* of trauma and loss? Or, to use a fancy philosophy term, what is the *teleology* of suffering? It's so easy to go from *describing* reality to *justifying* it. Suffering isn't there to make us awesome or fulfill God's Mystery Plan. It simply *is*.

But if God isn't actively making us suffer, isn't It in fact trying to *ease* our suffering? One of my favorite TV shows growing up, *Quantum Leap*, takes this idea in a sci-fi direction. Go into a room of nerds of a certain age and start reciting these opening words:

> Theorizing that one could time travel within his own lifetime, Doctor Sam Beckett stepped into the Quantum Leap accelerator *and vanished...* He woke to find himself trapped in the past, facing mirror images that were not his own, and driven by an unknown force to change history for the

> better. His only guide on this journey is Al, an observer from his own time, who appears in the form of a hologram that only Sam can see and hear. And so Dr. Beckett finds himself leaping from life to life, striving to put right what once went wrong, and hoping each time that his next leap will be the leap home...

People will start reciting it along with you, everyone getting goosebumps. It's sort of like a Nerd's Catechism. I don't know why it's so effective, this weird mixture of hope and Eighties hokeyness.

The "unknown force" is clearly supposed to be God, with Sam and Al often glancing up or pointing suggestively to the sky. Sam is a sort of guardian angel. In those moments of your life when you did something heroic, but you don't know how or why you did it—that was Sam "putting things right."

Let's leave aside the implications for free will (!) in this premise and think about *which* wrongs get put right. Sam has no control over where or why he Leaps. Ziggy the computer will infer the reason, though often Sam will ignore the computer and act on his own intuition. After fixing the problem that had originally gone wrong, Sam will Leap on to the next person. He saves a life, or stands up to a bully, or inspires someone.

Why does one person get Sam intervention while another doesn't? God seemingly Knows whom to send Sam to, and in a kind of grand butterfly effect, Knows which moments will have the most impact. But now God is making choices. *This* person's horrible mistake is worth fixing, but *that* person's accident is not. The act of withholding help is itself harm.

Quantum Leap is just a fun show, and it works emotionally, not literally. Maybe I shouldn't pick at it—but the show acts as a stand-in for how people think about God intervening in the world. What if God is enacting Its grand unknowable Plan, beautiful beyond the ken of humanity? Kusher has no patience for this end-justifies-the-means argument. Even if this Plan (which no one has seen) actually exists, it doesn't matter—there is no justification for the deaths of children, for the deaths of mothers, for all this suffering and loss.

God's pursuit of an ineffable, beautiful Plan reminds me of The Weaver, the insane omnipotent artist from *Perdido Street Station*. Its actions seem bizarre from the outside, but work according to an internal, inaccessible aesthetic sense — an army destroyed, or a flower left unplucked, or an ear cut off, were all the same in the end. One person's suffering fulfills the aesthetic requirements of the Universal Artwork and is allowed, while another's suffering does not—and is corrected.

A year before she died, during open enrollment at work, I looked at how much life insurance I had. I don't know why. I thought of how hard financially it would be for Polly if I died—and I realized there wasn't enough to cover both paying off the house and the expenses for a long period while she got on her feet. So I bumped it up, *way* up. Almost as an afterthought, unnoticed at the time, the policy notes that if your spouse dies instead of you, you will get half of the total coverage.

So I got a windfall, like winning an evil lottery. This is a sit-down-and-put-your-head-in-your-hands kind of co-incidence. Was Someone looking out for me, inspiring me to change my life insurance? Did Sam Leap into me, click around on the computer for a few minutes, and then Leap out? If there's a Force that could do such a thing, surely it could have inspired my wife not to get surgery, or woken me up at just the right moment in the middle of the night, or *done something* that could have prevented her death.

But isn't it more aesthetic this way, a more pleasing story beat for the audience? Justifying suffering on the basis of beauty is armchair philosophizing, disconnected from the pain of real life.

In the end, we say God "works in mysterious ways" because we're trying to map reasons onto a random process. There is no Hidden Plan.

Suffering doesn't "come from" anywhere. It doesn't forge you into a superhero. Pretending that suffering is actually good—either because it will make you awesome or because it is God's Will—only makes things worse. There is only how we choose to respond to it, how we pick up the pieces.

—which winter will
be the last—

the season has turned– sprinklers blown out– the
process of snow and dark preparation begun– the
harvest– the push of the seasons– and the red leaf–
sign– the end– the stop– the new cool air– that comes
suddenly with the slow plodding darkness– i'm trying to
clear the slate– a mindless listing of fall– the clichéd
transition– that doesn't affect everyone– and is deeper
the farther you travel from the equator– i didn't sleep
well last night– the weight of frustration– the power of
worry– we project our anxiety onto the squirrel– the
sense of impending scarcity– does the squirrel plan– or
count– or know which winter will be the last– like
knowing the ball will miss the pins by the feel of it
leaving your hand– why watch?– why did i sign up for

pain- am i duped by our culture?- a pawn of the sales
man?- wanting only what seems out of reach- or rare?-
why the shame around these things that are so common-
is the shame necessary- does it serve some purpose-
does it foster stronger relationships- more trial- are
you finished?- dropping the flow of writing- too
anxious- would i discover some compelling reason to get
off this particular conveyor belt- still distracting
myself with the contemplation of loss- the potential of
loss- the wishing to be a force that changes or alters
the loss for others- but bringing the insight that anger
doesn't listen- even as it compels confrontation- or a
giving over to the fate of others- that one cannot apply
one's own lessons to the expedient insight of others-
there is no warning to the heedless traveler- and even
so, one's rightness is contingent on the lottery of
events- it is frustrating that pain has so little meaning-
so little to teach us- it gets our attention- is there
some manifestation of life where pain does not evolve-
and would we experience anything that captures our
attention so completely as pain?- why do we describe
the sensations of physical and mental anguish in the
same way- does it, in fact, affect us the same way- we
have a myth that mental pain is ultimately worse- in its
lack of boundaries- but isn't it as circumscribed as
physical pain- contained in our minds- as the other is in
our bodies- and why do i go toward the pain- what
compels me?- what do i seek to learn there?- to atone
for there?- to prove there?- always understood as

seeking improvement despite the pain— there is no way
but through— but this surgery is not a given— there is
only one path that requires going through it— but the
pain is metaphorical— maybe it's socially constructed—
the idea that it is so painful not to be beautiful— that
any amount of physical pain is justified— here i go
again— to the altar of vanity— i am aware of the shame—

Do Not Go to the Altar of Vanity

(Letter sent to Boulder's Daily Camera *newspaper; never published.)*

This is a warning against plastic surgery. My wife Polly disparaged it as going to "the altar of vanity" and yet she went there and didn't come back. Her obituary was published in this newspaper almost a year ago on December 1, 2022.

Polly birthed three huge babies (the last one 10lbs) and her stomach was stretched out. Her official excuse was she wanted to fix her diastasis, but she also simply wanted a flat, youthful stomach again. She struggled with whether that was something she was allowed to want, this simple vanity. So she got an abdominoplasty (which goes by the nauseating nick-name "tummy tuck") and a week later she was dead.

The autopsy says it was due to natural causes, a "very large" clot right at the saddle where the arteries coming out of the lungs join together. No amount of CPR can help you if the oxygen from your lungs can't get to the rest of your body. I'm told that what happened is very rare, as if being an unusual statistic somehow puts it in perspective. I'm told that we did everything right (after the first day she was up and down a lot; by the end of the week we were taking short walks), as if the lack of guilt helps the loss.

But I am guilty. I could have told her not to go. She even asked me what I felt about it, because it's not very granola Boulder, is it, to modify your body this way. Was that an opening? Could I have vetoed it? I just wanted her to be happy, so I went along. And anyway, can you imagine—me "putting my foot down" like some kind of 1950s husband, with *this* woman?

This fierce feminist, this artist, this "fuck it, i'm polly" woman. It's ironic that this is what got her, the thing we worry about for our girls—that the magazine covers and the standard of beauty and the male gaze will burrow into their brains and distort them. The Male Gaze is like the Eye of Sauron, it "pierces cloud, shadow, earth and flesh." Even Polly wasn't immune.

Taking the kids to the pool and being around all the moms with suspiciously flat bellies definitely didn't help. Boulder isn't Miami. We have a story about ourselves that doesn't include plastic surgery, but I think it goes on quietly behind the scenes. Do the flat-bellied moms know how close it came, this bullet they dodged? They very nearly lost everything, and for what?

I don't have any research to back this up, but what do you think the proportion of women getting plastic surgery is versus the number of men? Two to one? Three to one? All these women, risking their lives, so that men can have some nice scenery. We men are not blameless here.

Neither is the plastic surgery industry. They sell a product—riskless body modification. I should have known, when the improbably handsome doctor came in, absurdly well dressed. You can't have ugly people sell you on beauty products, can you? Sure, they detail the risks—blood clots were explicitly called out. But contextualizing risk in our society is nearly impossible. Everything is risky, everything causes cancer, everything can cause injury and death. When everything is risky, nothing is risky. Is abdominoplasty riskier than, say, flying in an airplane? Driving a car?

We'll probably never know, because dying in recovery doesn't count. In the great pile of statistics, Polly's "natural causes" death won't be linked to her coincidentally having surgery six days earlier.

And the plastic surgery industry will roll on. They won't even notice you. The improbably handsome doctor will not call to offer his condolences. He's too busy letting the next woman risk her life.

So this is a warning. The risk isn't worth it. Mothers, stay with your children. You are beautiful, you know, just the way you are. Do not go to the altar of vanity.

you're always there, when I need you

—v secret—

(Draft of a letter never sent.)

Okay, Victoria's Secret, you say you're pivoting the brand. You have a new team of representatives who have creative input. I dare you to add me to the team. I'm not ashamed of my body. I'm aware of the complexities that exist between feeling comfortable and feeling sexy. I find your attempt to branch out with your brand identity interesting, but I don't see myself in it. So, let me tell you about me.

First, the salient points. I'm 42. 5'10." 170 lbs. I don't shave. I don't get my teeth whitened. I rarely wear makeup. I have multiple tan lines, warts, moles, skin tabs, pimples, stretch marks. I look like somebody who isn't a professional athlete or model. In fact, I look *like somebody's embarrassing mom.*

*I'm a SAHP (Stay-at-Home Parent) to three children.
I'm not actually in the market for a job, I just long to
stop thinking about my underwear. i want to stop thinking
about how it doesn't quite fit, how to wash and dry it
properly, where to possibly buy a bra I don't hate. I
wasn't always so hard to please; back in the day, I even
spent a summer steaming lingerie in the back room of a
Victoria's Secret.*

*My problems started when I aged out of the
twentysomething target demographic of the fashionable
end of fashion but failed to take on the apparently
ubiquitous apple shape of middle age that is catered
to, or acknowledged anyway, at the less fashionable end.
Oh, and I bore and nursed a few babies. Kudos on
acknowledging pregnancy as a potential state for
women's bodies, btw. There are actually quite a few
options out there for maternity and nursing, so I guess
it's great that you're getting into that game? It's the
post-nursing bra I can't seem to find. Something to
comfortably lift my little flaps up, maybe provide a
flattering, yet natural, shape. You know, a bra for the
many years of motherhood that come after the relatively
short pregnancy and nursing period.*

*Personally, I have no need to don tight, performance
enhancing clothes. I'm a walker, I can do that in jeans*

and a t-shirt. So, make your XXXXL athletic line and fill that niche in the market. Good for you.

Please, don't abandon the lingerie. Perhaps feeling sexy doesn't rate my to-do list as often as it used to. That's in part because it's begun to feel like a lofty goal, what with my perimenopausal libido and general exhaustion. You might be thinking maybe there are a few things i could do about that. Shave? Hormone therapy? But isn't the whole moving away from a singular idealized body type really about you coming to me? Isn't changing the models in your catalogues supposedly about idealizing me, as I am? So, if things like shaving and putting on makeup aren't my values; doesn't it become your challenge to develop looks that can make me feel sexy? Maybe that's too niche.

Anyway, I had written off Victoria's Secret years ago as an institution of my youth that no longer applied to me, maybe never did. I know you're trying to reflect just enough of the culture to sell more stuff, but you're doing that by pretending to be part of the conversation. I thought it worth asking, are you going to talk to me?

Wings and Horns

(Letter sent to the comic book Saga.*)*

D ear *Saga,*

My wife Polly died last year.

I'm now a sole father of three—Peggy, Hazel, and Cary. Don't get excited: Hazel was named after Hazel-rah, the Chief Rabbit in *Watership Down,* and not after your intrepid survivor Hazel.

That said, I've been reading *Saga* since before my Hazel was born, so maybe there's a little bit of your Hazel in my Hazel. Their ages have tracked pretty closely, as well as other parts of their life paths—like losing a parent.

I feel like I am Alana now. I didn't expect to find a role model in her as she tries to do right by her kids. I didn't expect any of this comic book to be relevant to me—it was just this gonzo sci-fi/fantasy head trip with gorgeous art. Sure it has death and loss, but that's just how you ground a crazy story, right? I didn't expect it to be about me.

I didn't expect to find relevance in the wings and horns. I'm an engineer (like the technological wings) and my wife was an artist (like the magical horns). We made babies together, and like Alana and Marko's Hazel they have curling horns coming out of their heads and iridescent wings spreading from their backs. They're the best of both of us, and are more than both of us.

I see my wife's face in their faces. I know what Alana feels when she looks at Hazel and sees Marko in there.

Hearing Hazel's adult voice narrate the story gives me hope, because that means she made it. I can sometimes hear my kids' future voices narrating our days. Maybe they will make it, too.

> Thanks for making this crazy comic,
> Aaron
> Boulder, CO

P.S. I'm also a little afraid to see where this whole spell to turn back time is going to go. I would give anything to go back in time and save my wife, but the hard truth is that it's literally impossible. If Hazel succeeds in this spell and brings back Marko, then…what is this story about, anyway? On the other hand, wanting to believe and trying anything in a desperate act of love is what grieving *is*. So maybe this is going in the right direction after all. I just have to trust in the process…

—dear amy—

(Letter to the advice column "Dear Amy," never published.)

Dear Amy,

I am a stay-at-home parent with small children. I appreciate your compassionate responses to parent criticism in general. I want to add to your response to "Concerned Grandparents" who wanted their kids to get off their phones and pay attention to their toddlers.

Some of the things I'm doing on my phone/tablet:

-Chatting with my husband, who's at work.

-Reading a book, news, parenting advice.

-Finding factual answers to my 5 year old's random questions.

-Emailing and texting. Keeping up friendships for

myself and my kids. Setting up playdates.
-Dealing with customer service.
-Making appointments.
-Banking.
-Writing and submitting this letter.
-Looking up medical symptoms to help me decide if my kid's latest cold necessitates taking the whole circus to Urgent Care.
-Researching home improvement projects.
-Control my thermostat, sprinklers, radio.
-Shopping— lots of shopping. Clothes, shoes, toys, appliances, groceries... just about anything.

I'd like these grandparents to consider, if you could have done all these things while your toddler played, continually sought your attention, and had tantrums in the privacy of your home instead of schlepping them around the department store, the hardware store, the bank, etc. and without the frustration of having telephone conversations constantly interrupted, would you have? Would you have found dividing your attention between your phone and kids a lesser evil?

Half-Double Grieving

That's me, silently crying in the children therapist's waiting room.

But it's not for the reasons you're thinking: I can't get this *god damn* crocheting hook into the right place.

With three kids in weekly therapy, I'm in that waiting room a lot. I'm using the time to slog through a "crochet block of the month club," where they send you yarn and instructions every month to make blocks that will assemble (eventually) into an afghan. Each block teaches a different stitch. Looking ahead, there's some really wild stuff. I'm still on the first block: single crochet (SC).

But first you have to make a chain (CH) *and I can't make it work*. My fingers don't know what to do. I've never done anything like this before. Once I'm done with the chain I'm supposed to stitch it *where*? When I bring the single-crochet row back along I'm supposed to insert the hook *where?*

The final afghan is 30 blocks, three blocks a month. I've been on this first block for three weeks. This is going to take *forever.* I'm never going to finish learning how to crochet. And if I never finish learning, I'm never going to finish Cary's blanket.

Polly was a list-maker. As I've gone through her sketchbooks and papers I've found them *everywhere.* They're little time capsules of our life from years ago: things she got done (or didn't get to) from some random week in 2014, or 2018, or 2021.

But there's one list that haunts me: her last list. It's full of projects she wanted to get done before surgery put her out of commission for a few weeks. Most of it was crossed off, like sewing the kids' Halloween costumes or finishing the custom street-address sign for our neighbor. But the top of the list was not yet crossed out: "Cary: Blanket."

Polly had a childhood crochet blanket made by her mom, which she passed along to Peggy, our first. Then for Hazel, our second, Polly designed her own blanket made of 200 multi-colored hexagons stitched together. For Cary she was in the process of crocheting a new blanket. She was 96 hexagons in. There are tubs of brightly colored yarn, ready to go.

I remember her working on it. We'd watch TV and she'd crank out those hexagons, one after the other.

I want to finish that blanket. I *need* to finish it.

After the first block, things get easier. I move on to double crochet (DC). Learning muscle memory from scratch is a strange thing. It's like learning how to walk, but with your hands. I can't say I'm any *good*, though. My second block is more of a trapezoid than a square. (Oh, you really *are* supposed to count!)

The nomenclature is bugging me. I don't understand the schema. When I get to the block teaching half double crochet (HDC), my engineer brain sees:

```
½ * 2 = 1
```

and balks, because it's also *not* true that:

```
1 HDC = 1 SC
```

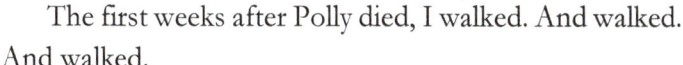

The first weeks after Polly died, I walked. And walked. And walked.

The kids were back in school, and my mom was there for when they came home. In the mornings I would fill a backpack with food and water, put on my hiking shoes and hat, and walk out the front door. I'd eventually hit a trailhead and follow it into the mountains. I didn't really care where the trail took me. Eventually I'd make it back home around dinner time.

I didn't have a clear idea of how far I was going on each hike. Looking at a map now, as best as I can tell I was pushing 18 miles a day in huge loops.

The hikes were not nearly long enough.

I say "hike" but it was more like "walking in a daze." The mountains were beautiful, but I only knew this intellectually. The photons of beauty entered my retinas and bounced off the cones and rods, but didn't make it to my brain. I was too consumed with the continuous loop going in my head to notice any beauty: My wife is dead. My wife is dead. My wife is dead.

When I get to "back-post treble crochet" (BPTR), I feel like I might actually know what I'm doing. The blocks are getting increasingly ambitious, and I realize that I'm learning stitches that aren't in Hazel's blanket.

Good: I don't want Cary's blanket to be my first one, all janky and first-timer. I need to have stitched thousands of times to build the muscle memory and technique, so that it looks *real*, so that my hexagons fit right in with Polly's, one of our last collaborations.

I do some back-of-the-envelope calculations: by the end, this blanket will have taken approximately 8,000 stitches. That sounds about right.

The first summer after Polly died, I drove. And drove. And drove.

I said yes to every invitation. I made some of my own. I piled the kids into the Subaru, threw stuff into the topper, got a dog-sitter, and took off. The vast emptiness of the summer days loomed, and I couldn't bear to be home. The kids were real troopers, and adapted well to 10-hour days driving across the plains. Having a Nintendo Switch helped.

I had to be out there, staring at the horizon.

I don't know what I thought about. The continuous loop was still going, though it had slowed down. There were moments when the kids would all be asleep in the middle of the day, and it was just me and the white noise of the tires on the asphalt. The automatic pilot in my head would keep the car on the road and I would feel my limerence for the dead and weigh how heavy emptiness can be.

But then they'd wake up and we'd blare music and make jokes and eat trashy road food. Our little team (Team Simmons) was on tour. They were with me and safe; I hadn't abandoned them in my grief. Something was stitching itself back together in my head.

With 30 blocks done, I whip-stitched them together into rows, and then brought the rows together, followed by huge loops of half-double crochet around the outside to bind it all together.

I looked at Hazel's blanket, and it's like I'd learned a new language—I could "read" it. I knew how it was put together. I'm standing where Polly stood, looking with her eyes, stitching with her hands.

Her stitches are tight and precise: I understand now

how good she was.

There are a lot of metaphors for grief, but the one I like best compares it to a kind of metabolism. With biological metabolism, you separate the nutrients from the waste, and incorporate the nutrients into your body. With grief you separate the horror and suffering from the love, passing out the waste as tears, and incorporate the love into your mind.

I didn't know it at the time, but the walking and the driving and the stitching were my metabolic process. I was (and still am) metabolizing the grief into a simple fact that I can hold in my hand and recite with a straight face and dry eyes: my wife is dead.

There's one last new stitch to learn right at the end, a reverse single crochet (RSC) round to give it a nice framing. It's awkward and crab-walky, but I adapt quickly and have it down pat after five or so stitches.

It's all in a pile in my lap and I round the very last round. I cry as I finish it, in a new kind of disbelief. I never thought I'd get this far. This blanket was supposed to just be a way-stop to Cary's blanket—I had been calling it the "janky blanky," not taking it seriously, only seeing its first-timer flaws. I never thought it would be an object in itself. Who is the blanket even for, now that it's done? The answer follows the question, instantly.

It's for Polly. This is Polly's blanket.

Next up: 100+ multicolored hexagon blocks to go with the ones that Polly already made. They look like some variation on stitches in a round, sort of like a granny square. (I call them "granny hexes," which sounds like a magic spell.) I try out some hexagon patterns I find online, but they don't look like hers. I'm not quite sure how she made these, or even what the stitch is, but I can see the path forward. I know now that it's something I can learn. Maybe I can ask someone at a yarn store. I know the language, after all. I know how to ask crochet questions and understand the answers.

It's taken me a while to get here. A year to get my brain back, and another year to learn how to crochet. But now I'm finally ready to cross that item off Polly's list.

—imagine a hallway—

this is an idea— a study for what is a much larger
piece— this is my first attempt to "speak" through art
concretely— in a somewhat literal approach to
feminism— ultimately, i imagine a hallway full of faces
that flicker and move with the breeze created by the
viewer— hands that wave, that continue to move and
build— bells that ring— creating the chatter of a
population that is not resigned to the "reality" (socially
constructed) that they are born into— a population that
is not resigned to representation in statistics— a
population that is acutely aware of its past— of its
predecessors— who refuses to be content with the same
old struggles generation after generation— a population
bent on building on itself— of recognizing greatness in
its rare occurrences— on avoiding the seduction of
laziness— easy comfort— this population demands

society to offer opportunities to those who will take
them- rewards hard work not only in the public sphere-
but in every sphere that hard work is done in- how do
we begin to evaluate worth without the use of money- and
then, if your value to the community doesn't translate to
your ability to care for yourself and your family- then
what is it worth?- how can value have any other
meaning?- how can contribution have any other
payment?- the creation of identity- and how i have
sought to contribute to that conversation through my
work- and does it have any value until someone else
assigns value to it through verbal translation- it
sometimes seems to make more sense to make only
aesthetic statements- so they may, at best, be
translated poorly- installation and performance are at
least manipulative artforms- paintings are a bit
removed- and when they are emotive they seem to lack
the intellectual- or it must be explained- by some
other medium- i am putting off housework now-

Polly's Reading List

I go on long walks and sometimes Polly is walking with me and sometimes she isn't. Anyway, I think about things. One thing I thought of was "Polly's Reading List," if you want to get into her head or feel her reading over your shoulder:

Life Is Hard by Kieran Setiya

The last thing she read. We talked about this book at length on our walks, and it was on my list to get to. I'm reading it presently.

What does an atheist moral framework look like? How do we pass on our values to our kids? This problem preoccupied Polly, because while the organized religions seem to have solved how to transmit things to our kids, what they're transmitting is problematic. On the other hand, secular moral philosophy is often dry, abstract, and haughty. This book asks, "What would a philosophy look like that was tested in the crucible of direct moral experience?"

Fair Play by Eve Rodsky

Guys, you need to read this before your wife does. It's not for you (it's going to make you defensive) but it is about you. It's about how you're not doing enough. It's about how your wife is complicit in letting it happen. This is where the rubber meets the road with feminism. A lot of books complain about the problem of the domestic workload, but this is the only one that offers practical guidance on how to actually fix it.

Watership Down by Richard Adams

One of Polly's favorites—the ending always made her cry. Hazel's name comes from this book.

A story about cute little bunny rabbits this is not. It's violent and mystical and heroic. It's about a band of rabbits fleeing from the destruction of their warren to found a new one, and the hero's journey of Hazel into their leader, Hazel-rah. I've been thinking a lot about mythological manifestations of Death, and this book has a great one—the Black Rabbit of Inlé.

Lonesome Dove by Larry McMurtry

I think Polly loved this book because her mother did, and it was a way for her to feel connected. But it's also tremendous. McMurtry supposedly set out to subvert the western, and accidentally created a foundation stone for the genre.

Clara Allen's speech near the end of the book about why she didn't marry Augustus was something that resonated with Polly.

For a quick fix, watch the old '80s miniseries with Robert Duvall.

A Heartbreaking Work of Staggering Genius by David Eggers

Polly lost her mother when she was in high school. Eggers lost both his parents when he was not much older. This memoir is raw and hilarious and all over the place. It was one of the first books we read out loud to each other. I think Polly saw herself in it, and the possibility of being able to make something out of the energy of grief.

Birthing From Within by Pam England and Rob Horowitz

This book prepares women for childbirth, giving you psychological tools to deal with not just pain but with the unexpected. It was where Polly came across the distinction between pain and suffering. The book's approach isn't just limited to childbirth, and led to Polly's famous (to us) aphorism, "expectations cause suffering."

—the prom—

water drips from the end of the hose a good half a minute
after the faucet is turned off— sometimes i'm not patient
enough to let it finish— i grab the pail and let the
trickling water spatter the floor— there's no harm done—
the floor is cement and the walls are cement blocks
halfway up— the top half is a two by four frame covered
with miscellaneous pieces of corrugated aluminum— there
is a gap at the top of the walls where the frame meets
the roof— the bathroom is a haven for mosquitoes— not that
they don't enjoy the rest of the house— i am heating water
to bathe— i am filling a tub half full of cold water from
the tank outside the bathroom— the light socket is broken
because i tried to put an outlet/socket in it and broke
it in the process— i am holding a small, but heavy, metal
maglight in my mouth as i fumble between a craftsman rip-
off and a medium swiss army knife to replace the broken

socket- the wire is solid copper wire that resists reshaping and is stubbornly resisting finding its place under the screw- i smell gas and realize the light has gone out on the burner- i relight it singeing my hand in the process- i am thinking about what i can make for dinner in as little time possible- i eventually get the wire to cooperate- the new socket in place and working- the water heats and i bathe while boiling linguine- i decide what to wear and what to dress my pasta with simultaneously- i am only an hour late for the prom and i feel pretty good about it –

Taking Back the Lie Dream

It should have been Neil Gaiman's death (that happy goth) who came for her, but it wasn't. It was the Christian Devil, with the horns and the fire and the malice.

"Look at you lying there," he sneered. "Even after the two loud thumps when you fell, he hasn't come to see you. Oh, he woke up and wondered what it was. He even came up the stairs and stared into the darkness, waiting for the child to cry out who must have fallen out of bed. But when no sound came he went back down."

The Devil paced back and forth, staring at her body.

"And now! He whacks off in the bathroom, trying to be quiet and not wake you."

The Devil listened for a moment.

"And now he's up, making coffee and thinking about work. He's even getting out the laptop and trying to fix that White Whale bug that he's been on about. God, he just *wouldn't stop talking about it*, would he?"

The Devil started pacing again.

"He wasn't even with you when it happened! Oh, you told him to sleep downstairs because of his God-awful snoring, but, really, shouldn't he have insisted he stay with you? Shouldn't he have been here for this moment? Shouldn't he have *saved* you?"

The Devil looked at his watch.

"He won't find you for another two hours! He's not even thinking about you. He doesn't love you, he never loved you. It was only what you could do for him that was important. He was selfish and defensive and he didn't love you. Look, your body is starting to grow cold."

The Devil stopped pacing.

"It's time to go, now. There's nothing for you here."

The Devil put his hands on his hips.

"What, you're not coming? You can't stay here."

The Devil tapped his hoof impatiently.

"Fine. Disperse into nothingness, believing that he loved you. It's far better than being tortured by me, for no reason, forever."

The Devil vanished in a swirl of brimstone. The body, now empty, lay there, waiting.

—ways to kill time—

101 ways to kill time
1. write a novel
2. stare at the wall
3. make a mess
4. clean it up
5. watch pot boil in a non-metaphorical sense
6. wait— wait for life to start— for dreams to come true— hope— get through the day
7. learn to solve crosswords
8. sing
9. write poems no one will ever read, songs no one will ever hear
10. be relieved you're not contributing anything negative to the world through your lack of contribution
11. count your fears
12. count your blessings
13. remain single
14. become entangled in a romantic relationship that

lacks the potential to grow and change
15. volunteer for the peace corps
16. make your own 150alloween costume
17. do laundry
18. make your bed
19. lower expectations
50 ways to kill time
20. dream
21. sleep in late- morning time lasts much longer than evening time
22. only begin once you've found the perfect sentence

i'm stuck on beginnings- it's the end i cannot imagine- the coming to a single conclusion about anything- even if it's totally made up- i guess i'm a hamlet kind of tragedy- completely unoriginal- and yet i still speak- still think- still try to capture the melody found in ambience- or something like it

i fear i have nothing to say- or no unique- thereby valuable- way to say it- i'm paralyzed- i cannot conceive of an interesting car wreck- for my life has been blessed- i am an artist of confusion and convolution- i understand the basic concepts of literature but do not know how to find them in my own life
it's an animated movie about a donkey that shits and vomits gold- you remember the story- the gold ass and lying goat-

perhaps i should begin after death- instead- and call afterdeath a kind of blood substance that is physically present in the throats of the bereaved and can only be dislodged by wailing- here is my wail song-

All You Pollies

I make sure Polly's email account is clear. I check it every few days, and aggressively unsubscribe, close out accounts, and report spam. I don't know why I do this. Perhaps it's the same impulse as sweeping a gravestone free of leaves, of bringing fresh flowers to the mausoleum.

Perhaps I'm expecting an email from a long lost friend who somehow doesn't know, and I don't want them to think she's not replying. But it's more than that—a new email in her inbox feels like a violation. Someone is calling her name who shouldn't be. It's supposed to be quiet in there.

What's worse is getting emails *from* Polly on that account.

When it first happened I thought I was hallucinating. The Hilton in North Platte, Nebraska seemed to think she'd stayed there a few days ago:

Guest Name:	POLLY SIMMONS
Guests:	1 Adult
Rooms:	1
Room Plan:	1 KING BED
Your Rate Information	HONORS DISCOUNT
Rate per night	130.66 USD
Total for Stay per Room Rate	130.66 USD

When people say, "I can't believe she's dead," they usually mean it metaphorically. For a long time I meant it literally. I held her body and I still didn't believe it. I expected people to demand proof from me—how were they so easily accepting my story about her death?

What if… she faked her death? She took one of those drugs that slows down your metabolism, makes it only *seem* like you're dead. (Does a drug like that even exist, or is it like "truth serum"?) She bribed the EMTs to go along with it. She had to get away from me at all costs, like Julia Roberts in *Sleeping With the Enemy*. I could be the villain, if that meant she was alive somewhere.

Polly made a mistake, though. She stayed in that hotel and absent-mindedly gave her old email address. And the receipt had her address in a remote town in South Dakota.

I could drive up there and walk to the front door. I'm not actually the villain, you see. What really happened was she just couldn't take being a mother and wife anymore— it was too much, she had to reinvent herself so she could make art all day.

I could knock on that door, and she'd open it, covered in paint, paint on her cargo pants, paint on her glasses, paint on her cheek. Her hands are white from plaster, or maybe dried concrete. Her hair is matted with sawdust. She's beautiful. She's not even surprised to see me, but relieved. We kiss and the door closes, and the movie fades to black.

The emails keep coming, though. Often it's a receipt from a store. Sometimes it's a hotel itinerary. There have even been emails from match-making services. Other home addresses and phone numbers. Other Pollies.

How do they not know their own email addresses?

Another fantasy unrolls itself in front of my eyes. I could drive to *all* their houses. Like the Terminator going down the list of Sarah Conners, but again I'm not the villain. I just want to look in the faces of all you Pollies, and make sure mine isn't hiding among you.

And I'd also deliver a polite PSA: Please, *for the love of God*, start using your own email address.

—the struggle—

so the idea that you can't control the future— but can
you train a dog?— not children— but there must be
something to say for habit— habitual thinking— does
identity affect behavior— what is identity if not
behavior— i think they might be very different things—
what is a good parent— a parent who identifies as a good
parent?— if we could dismiss this idea of parenting
today, would that really affect how we approach it?—
how we feel about it?— if we are reaching toward
grace— i need a new word— if self-consciousness is
essential for self-awareness— then aren't we going to
necessarily feel judged?— what is success?— and
good?— and better?— biology etc, seems to paint us as
limited beings, like dogs— more like dogs than
transcendent consciousness— omnipotent gods— are we at
an advantage because we can imagine omnipotence—

because we desire omnipotence- woman's tattoo said
"there will be an answer"- what does that mean?- is that
a threat? a promise? a faith?- "and there will be more
questions"- though death does seem to hold a kind of
terrifying finality- and "there will be no more
questions"- that is the promise i see in death- there
will be nothing to ask then- for some of us the pain and
struggle of the question is what defines us- without it
we cease to exist- but every moment isn't a struggle-
there are many moments throughout the day that are
defined by peace- not struggle- i guess you could
strive toward that- the struggle is so much more
interesting to me- not in a faux struggle way- choosing
to suffer- but i prefer to look at, express the pain-
sometimes that leads to suffering- but, yeah, suffering
happens, too- it gets old- i get it- sometimes you don't
see it coming- you charge into it- you figure out how to
get out- you eat- and you still figure out how to get
out- you accept help- you fail- and you figure out what
to do next- what do you learn- what do you think you
learned?- failure helped me follow the ordinary path-
i can see the success of that choice- but sometimes i...-
a lot of the time- i dream-

I Still Dream of Krypton

I am watching Richard Donner's 1979 *Superman: The Movie* with the kids. Polly is in surgery. We're all nervous and biding our time.

Lex Luthor launches two nuclear warheads in opposite directions. Superman throws one into space, but doesn't get to the second one in time. He still manages to save everyone, everyone but Lois Lane, whose car is swallowed into a crack in the earth, dirt bursting into the car like it was underwater, and she drowns in dirt, gasping. Superman finds her, seconds too late, pulls up the car and rips off the door. He sets her body down, gently, sobbing.

That scene has always touched me, Christopher Reeve is really grieving, and now I'm wondering if I should be watching this, if I'm seeing Polly's death. What if she doesn't make it out of surgery?

Then Superman rages—it's terrifying—and he rockets

161

into the sky. Jor-El appears to him with his one admonition, "It is forbidden to interfere in human history," but Kal-El doesn't care. He flies around the Earth as fast as he can to make it spin backwards and time reverses (!), and it's cheesy as hell, but then again they're channeling the Silver Age comics, aren't they? It rides that line between ridiculous and awesome perfectly.

Then Superman flies the other way, and time moves forward and Lois doesn't die. He lands, and she's standing by the car, impatient and complaining at him. All Superman can do is beam at her. He's saved Lois, that's all that matters.

I get the text that Polly made it out of surgery. I leave to pick her up.

I am reading the original 1970s *World Of Krypton* by Kupperberg and Chaykin. We are at the cabin. It is years ago; we are in the past. Polly is in her chair, doing the crossword. The kids are drawing. It is snowing outside.

In one of the stories, the Kryptonians had a computer called "matricomp" that through its superior match-making skills prevented divorce from becoming a planetary scourge (social preoccupations of the 70s much?). Jor-El and Lara are matched (and destined to bear Kal-El), but matricomp falls in love with Lara and tries to kill Jor-El before they can dismantle it.

It is so bad and cracks me up so much, I read it out loud to the kids, but really I'm reading it to Polly and the groans and eye-rolls are wonderful.

I am watching the 1990's *Superman: The Animated Series* with the kids. The show is silly and fun, and has nothing to do with my life.

Then Lois Lane falls through a dimensional portal (as you do) and finds herself in a dystopian Metropolis ruled over by a despotic authoritarian Superman. Superman is stunned to see her, and we find out that in this world, Lois has died. Superman in his despair has gone completely off the rails.

Superman is not dealing with his grief well. He is not experiencing "post traumatic growth."

I go to work, and I am Superman. Because of my powers with computers, I am made a big deal of. Free unlimited fountain Cokes! Surprise bonuses! Giant raises! Constant praise!

Who can withstand such bounty without getting an inflated ego, a super ego even? The real Superman somehow never lets all this go to his head—he must have super-humility. I do not have this power.

Meanwhile, at home, Polly is Supergirl—she moves Heaven and Earth and no one notices. Her homeworld exploded when she was 18 when her mother died. Sometimes you can see the sadness, but mostly it motivates her to be the best mother she can be. To be there with her children all the more fiercely because her own mother can't.

I am reading Moore and Swan's 1980's *Whatever Happened To The Man Of Tomorrow?* I've read enough grief books. It's time for something to distract myself. Moore's Superman stories are some of the best; let's re-read one.

The time-traveling Legion of Superheroes arrives with 1960s Supergirl in tow. Superman is shocked and can't believe what he's seeing because… because Supergirl *died* just a few months earlier in *Crisis on Infinite Earths*. Oh, that's right. I'd completely forgotten. That was such a big deal at the time—Superman on the cover holding Supergirl's dead body, crocodile tears streaming down his face, all the other dumbfounded heroes on the margins.

Supergirl wants to know how things are going with her future self, and where is she? Oh, she must be time-traveling. Superman can't lie to her, but he also can't tell her the truth, so he tells her, that's right, Supergirl's not here, that she's in the past.

She's in the past.

My homeworld exploded when I was 45. In the fiery destruction I stuffed my children and my dog into a rocket ship hastily assembled. We careened through space, through supernovas, through Saturn's rings, with John Williams music blaring. The rocket crashed into the Earth and we climbed out of the wreckage.

People beheld us and were amazed! Earth's yellow sun had given us powers. "How is it that you can walk and talk and laugh and cry like ordinary humans?" Even we didn't understand at first.

I am reading King and Everly's 2021 *Supergirl: Woman Of Tomorrow*. This story is sort of "True Grit" with space pirates, where Supergirl is John Wayne, protecting a young girl who's on a vengeance quest for her murdered father.

They go over Kara Zor-El's origin from a new angle—one emphasizing how awful it must have been for her. Kal-El had it easy, as he was just a baby and has no memories of Krypton or his parents; the loss is abstract. But for Kara it's all too real, as she was a teenager when Krypton exploded. Kara's ability to be super-good is even more impressive given her background. She *remembers*.

At the climax of the story, when the girl has captured her father's killer and is about to kill him in turn, an exhausted, demoralized Kara gives up, admitting that she can't stop the girl from exacting her revenge. Who is Kara to tell this girl to let go of her grief for her father, when Kara herself can't let go of her grief for her own parents, for Krypton itself? Even now, after all this time, Kara still dreams about Krypton.

I want to go on a Quest. I want to find a cave and descend into Hades. I want to fly into Space. I want to travel through Time. I want to punch God in the mouth. I want to make a deal with the Devil. I want to outwit

Death in a game of chance. Like Orpheus, like Gilgamesh, like Luthien. Like Superman.

At night I look at the stars, where you can still see the light from Rao, Krypton's red sun. I think of the life we had, our house while Polly was in it, the future we thought we had together.

My homeworld is gone. My kids and I are trying to create a new one.

But I still dream of Krypton.

—my mind is alive—

my mind is alive— i cannot sleep— you proposed— in your sweet way— shy and unassuming— and it was wisely private— i like it being a private moment— the wedding will be public enough— there are so many opportunities for art— it's hard to know where to start— it's hard to approach it as a collaboration— after all my big talk— so many questions— my god— is it real?— will it be be more real when i have a ring?— will it be less?— this long awaited fantasy— i don't know how you can sleep— and yet i wish i could— so i could wake up tomorrow and be revived— i'm sorry i've been hurt the last few days— it happens— where, when, how— at least the why and who have answers— finally some answers— it will be a bit frustrating— i know, contemplating these questions with you— me for the millionth time, you for the first— but there's time to let it sink in for you— maybe you waited

till now to ask so that it'd be more than a year- but i
always throw the curve- how am i going to tell my
family?- it seems like such an awkward thing to do-
how do i tell my friends- it feels like old news
somehow- i wanted to cry when you asked me- but you
took me by surprise- i wasn't even paying attention to
you- i should have known something was strange when you
got upset about the tv's- and kept remarking on how it
wasn't what you had in mind- this is our life together-
these are our things- i wish i felt tired- but i'm
pumped full of adrenaline- it's been so long since i've
written anything- it feels foreign- you'd think this
page would wear me out- i'm in a good place- a nice
place- i've made it mine- and i hope you like it- it's
not as late as i feared- some talents i do not possess- i
don't know if i hear you stirring or not- i hope not- it's
not my intention to disturb you- it's to write out this
excitement so i can drift off to sleep-

The Butt-Dial of Destiny

Do you remember? I remember. I worry that if I don't remember it will never have happened.

I was on the 12-hour ferry from Manila to Coron, the middle leg of the epic (but now mundane) trek back to my site on the far side of Busuanga Island, Palawan Province, Philippines.

That trek! Later, I would make it so often to come see you, concocting excuses like running a computer training for your teachers, or helping you put together those mud ovens.

Get up at four in the morning (behold the stars from my tiny island town!). Ride the three-hour open-window bus to Coron (surprisingly cold for a tropical island). Wade a roaring river or two if it's rainy season (the bridges were too weak to hold an overloaded bus). Wait a day in Coron for the ferry time. Sleep on the ferry overnight in one of those rooms with twenty bunks. Arrive in Manila, cab to the bus station. Wait for the bus. Ride the six-hour bus to Baguio City (the aircon is intense, make sure to bundle up). Get on the much jankier bus for the twisty, cliff-side, car-sick, beautiful, 8-hour ride to Besao. Confuse the bus-driver that you're not getting off at Sagada, the typical tourist destination. Get off in little Besao, walk up the terraces to your tin-roof shack on the mountainside. That tin-roof shack that you nested into a home. The place I wish I could time-travel back to, nowadays.

But I'm getting ahead of myself. That hasn't happened yet. I was on the ferry heading *back*. We had just gotten together, after that education conference in Tagaytay. We had that date in Malate. I had boldly booked a room at the pension instead of a bunk. We kissed. We slept together. I resisted sex (residual Catholicism?), which confused and intrigued you. We had to go back to our sites. Busuanga Island for me, my tiny dot of ink on the globe, just north of Palawan Island. Besao for you, nestled in the rice-terraced Mountain Province of northern Luzon. So I was on the ferry, not overnight in this direction, but still in a bunk.

And then the ship's engine broke.

It suddenly got real quiet, out there on the open ocean. The ship began to freely drift, turning with the waves, and began to bob along with them. Oh, *that bobbing*. I couldn't stand up for more than five minutes without getting extremely sea sick. I lay in my bunk for hours, listening to music, smelling the paint (they decided this was a good time to paint the walls). I would get up, dash to the bathroom, hurry to the commissary, eat as fast as possible, say hi to the Navy ex-pat having a beer (who was clearly at home in this situation), speed-walk back to the bunk.

I don't remember how long this went on. Thirty hours? As we drifted west into the South China Sea, eventually a tugboat was dispatched from Manila and slowly got to us. It docked, turned us into the waves (oh thank god, I can stand up again), and chugged us back to Manila. I heard later that we made the ABS-CBN news. There were always stories about ships floundering, overcrowded, hundreds of Filipinos drowning. Ours was a happy ending. Assuming the tug could get us back to Manila.

When we finally got within sight of land (don't get excited: still maybe a day to go), our cellphones began to pick up signal. I could text you. Regale you with my tale, in little blobs of textese shorthand.

Then you called me.

At first I was confused. I could hear your voice, muffled and distant, but you wouldn't answer my hello. I could hear other voices, slightly more distant. What was going on? Oh, this is a butt-dial. This happens all the time—my double-A at the top of everyone's contact list, a quirk of an ancient name colliding with modern times.

Normally I would just hang up, but it was you, so I tried to get your attention. But you were too busy talking. Talking about me.

I'm not a nosy person. I don't eavesdrop, or look at other people's emails. I didn't plant a bug. But this was too much narcissism for even an ordinary person. I should have hung up, but I didn't. I started to listen.

"I don't know. I like him, but I think he might be *too nice*." What the hell? Was this you ginning yourself up for a breakup? Or, more weirdly, did you call me *on purpose* so that I would hear this and take the hint?

I hung up and texted you, angry, why not just tell me directly instead of this weird game?

I obviously didn't yet know you very well, did I? Of all people, there's no way you would do something passive-aggressive like that. You're *direct*. If anything, you're aggressive-aggressive. You were just trying to work things out in your head, bouncing things off some other volunteers. I think maybe you were afraid of what was happening between us.

You saw the text, horrified, and called me. We talked. We figured it out. Since I was boomeranging back to Manila, we made plans to meet up "halfway" in Baguio City.

And something changed between us. I had stood up for myself; I didn't roll over. I had started an argument. I wasn't *nice*. There was integrity in here, too; it's not all "friendly nerd." And that was all you needed. You needed to know that if you pushed against me, I could push back.

Do you remember where we stayed in Baguio? Hotel 45, that hovel, with the room barely big enough for its bed, a tiny camo TV in the corner by the ceiling, that adjunct closet bathroom with the ungrounded water heater on the shower head. That love nest.

Two, three times a day, for days on end. Eventually my plumbing wore out. I even, embarrassingly, *cried* out of disappointment in myself for not being able to just go on and on. You thought it was sweet, and hilarious, and teased me about it for years afterward.

That call on the ship, I marvel at the improbability of it. Would we have stayed together, without that push to reveal our characters?

When God with His right hand arranged that Butt-Dial of Destiny, was He with His left hand also arranging the molecules of your blood so that they would clot that day far in the future?

When we came back to the States, it was like the front door was open and we just walked through, holding hands. Everything broke our way, for years. You can get used to good luck, too easily. Was there a finite store of it? Did we recklessly draw it down to empty?

I'm supposed to say that it's worth the pain of grief for having gotten to know you. If I could send a message back to us right after the butt-dial, would we have continued on in full knowledge? I think you might have; you're strong that way. You would have looked at me with those blue eyes and those dimples and said with your sultry voice, "Come on." We'd have walked through the front door of our future again, holding hands.

—christmas was hot
this year—

for christmas, i went down to aaron's place—his mother
and sister came for their visit—

christmas was hot this year— the post card picture you
have in your mind of the tropical beach getaway—
turquoise water and white sand beaches— conveniently
edits out the grit of sand perpetually on your hands,
the humid stickiness of the air, the salt taste of the
water— and the fact that there's not a whole lot to do at
the beach besides wait until you can go home and take a
shower— i know i'm being rather close minded— suffice
it to say, i think i'm cured of the tropical beach
fantasy—

we went snorkeling one day- that was stressful- took me
all day to stop holding onto the boat for a few feet-
but i feel good about my few feet- i did have the
sense, however, that though the coral was cool and the
fish fun to see, humans do not belong there- aaron's all
excited that i tried it- said we could get me a good
snorkel- yeah, babe, i wouldn't go that far...- i spent
most of the day fantasizing about teaching aaron to ski-
i'm not above a little vengeance- maybe i'll politely
suggest he try wearing a life vest, see how he takes it-

i think aaron got his fill of catering to women, anyway-
can't say that i was much help, really- we went to a
beach near aaron's site that had these little bugs living
in the sand- i mean they were everywhere- they started
biting me as soon as we got there- by noon, i was done-
done, done- and done- hot, sticky, sandy, salty AND
ITCHY?- no- so i left them and walked- maybe did a
little stomping- through the midday sun- afterwards,
i'm talking the next week and a half, we all itched like
crazy- the kind of itching that you absently start and
cannot stop- it was fun-

for all my bitching, i enjoyed the trip- coron was much
cooler than when i last visited- but still hot enough to
make the constant power outages (that is, the fans stop
working) lend a certain misery to it i am simply not
accustomed to, living here in my cool, even cold,
mountain abode- and once again, it helped me feel

better about my placement— even if it means i don't have any little girls in my life here that come close to the sweetness of aaron's host sisters—

someday, i might tell you about new year's in manila— but i'm still shell shocked from all the fire crackers— filipinos go for the noise rather than visual effect— i don't mean measly little black cats, either— mom would have LOVED it—

Many folk like to know beforehand what is to be set on the table; but those who labored to prepare the feast like to keep their secret; for wonder makes the words of praise louder.

-Gandalf

Than Never To Have

I don't know why I went to Polly's funeral.

Excuse me, "Celebration of Life." I don't know why people are afraid to use the word "funeral," when that's clearly what it was. Okay, yes, it was in an art museum and not a funeral home. I don't think a traditional venue would have been able to cope with the amount of artwork they put up. An art museum was definitely "on brand," you could say. Anyway, even if they'd used the right word it was surely non-traditional.

Just like her wedding was. I don't know why I went to that, either.

I was surprised I even got an invite to the wedding, to be honest. I suspect it was because I was part of the RPCV crew, and I lived in Colorado, and it would've been weird *not* to invite me. You know how wedding invitations get.

So, yeah, we dated back in Peace Corps. There was

just something about her, this sparky chemistry we had right from the beginning. She was so *sure* of where she wanted our relationship to go, talking about marriage *really* early. I guess it freaked me out a little, though I rolled with it for a while. And then the end of service loomed, and the return to the Real World bore down on us.

Was all this just a dream? Were either of us making rational decisions? I mean, I regularly rode on top of jeepneys along with all the other Filipinos as if it were the most natural thing to do, but try that once you're stateside and see what happens. Was our relationship like that? Did it only make sense there, in the Peace Corps time-warp?

I also don't have the best examples of marriage working out. I and everyone I knew seemed to have divorced parents. Maybe marriage was untenable, a myth. Though if you're living together, own a house together, have children together… does it matter whether there's a marriage certificate? Aren't you, in fact, married? But even if we used the right word, I wasn't sure that's what I wanted, or was capable of having.

Polly made the hard pitch for marriage. She just looked at it differently. It was just something you did, with integrity, in front of everyone. She wanted to go through something hard with a partner (like having kids) and look back and say, we did this together. It was very compelling. I imagined what living with an artist like her would be like, the house decorated wildly, full of art. What would it be like to live with a partner with such integrity, who took marriage so seriously?

But then I chickened out. I broke up with her, worried that I would screw it up later if I let it go stateside, so let's end it now. "Aaron," she said, "don't." But I was stubborn, and she wasn't one to beg. I thought I knew what I wanted.

So off we went in different directions. I wound up getting a job in Colorado and lived just down the way. She met some doof and married him. I never saw her. She didn't believe in being friends with exes, and that was just as well.

I got deep into my career. I dated women, but nothing ever quite worked out. I was too cynical. I always had a foot out the door.

And then, years upon years later, I got The Call. Polly was gone. I should say "dead," but I can't. Does it matter what word I use?

I went to the funeral, and I watched the doof give his eulogy. And then I watched their *children* (the youngest was five) give a eulogy, followed by people from every phase of Polly's life.

There was art on the walls from Polly's MFA days. There were collaborations with her kids. There were casts of her pregnant belly. There were 3x3 black-and-white grids of baby faces. There was *so much*.

During the reception, people ate and drank, laughing, and children ran underfoot. It was… just like her wedding. Full of art. Full of children. Full of *kama muta*. Full of life.

I watched her widower, the doof, move through the crowd, talking to everyone. I avoided him. How can I be envying this man, obviously in such pain? Maybe because he's not a doof anymore. That's what marriage to Polly had done to him, what having a life partner like her had done. And I had thrown it away.

I stumbled out of the museum before it was over, disoriented. I walked around the neighborhood, struggling to understand. I had never been happy. I had never had a purpose in my life. The doof has lost everything! But he had a purpose. Even with her gone, he had a purpose. And here I am, so fucking smart: lost.

I wish I could go back, and listen to Polly's marriage pitch, *really* listen. And do the brave thing and say... yes.

There's a phrase, one of those pat aphorisms, but I'm having trouble remembering the right words. It's there on the tip of my tongue. *Better to have loved and...* something. I'm sure it'll come to me.

—married—

confusion, information overload, overstimulation,
frustration, complexity, responsibility, freedom,
expansion, identity, identity formation, self-awareness—
truth, necessity, commodification— modernity— self-
criticism, overwhelming, destiny, social contribution,
honesty, integrity, fiction, reality, self, improvement,
duality, language, isolation, beauty, the purpose and
function of art, torn, ambiguity, ambivalence, experience,
personal vs universal, faith, determination, craft,
concept, hierarchies, priorities, value system—
individuality, taking for granted, media— i am now
married—

For the Newlyweds

"Till death do us part" isn't true.

It sounds romantic and grand, but it just isn't true. The two ways out of marriage may be death and divorce, but that's not the end. There has been no parting.

Polly is still in my life. I talk to her. I go on walks with her. I see her face in our children. I'm surrounded by her creations. I live in the house that she made. I read her words in her journal, where she talks to me.

I Speak for her.

In *Ender's Game*, Orson Scott Card imagines a new religion organized around Speakers for the Dead. That's what it feels like—Polly is silent, but I am her voice, her representative on earth. It is my responsibility to keep her flame alive, like prehistoric man keeping the fire going in the cave.

This is not how we usually understand our wedding

vows. The vows refer to the obligations of life (richer and poorer, respect and love), but they don't mention the obligations of death. They're at best implied; a lemma buried in the text.

I want to replace "Till death do us part" and make it explicit: "Will you Speak for me when I am dead?"

Whether you know it or not, this is what you've signed up for. It can seem like a real downer to point this out to newlyweds, in this brand-new context of life and hope, with your lives laid out before you—one of you will die and leave the other.

But you need to enter into this with full knowledge that death will come. Like the Norse gods, who know that they will die in Ragnarok, *but choose to fight anyway.* To love is to defy death.

So live. Love each other. Have children, whose faces will be a mix of you both.

And Speak for your spouse when they're gone.

—love is the path of resistance—

the girl walked up the road— dirt— and full of rocks—
the bus would come down it— cement— stairs curving
between cinderblock and still sheet houses— rust and
grey— some painted pastels— the trash made into
planters— never winter here— the road thwarted by the
constant growth— by the ground constantly changed by
rain— everything flows— she walked up the stairs to the
road— and the road until it became dirt— and through
the forest of pines— she listed to the breeze in the
needles— and felt less far from home— but she couldn't
leave the path— the road— because she was not home—
and the ground didn't hold you here— unless you knew
it— so she listened for home— and walked the road—
feeling a little freer— than in her house— that nestled

among houses of neighbors she'd never know- but who
knew of her- on the road she was alone- she had
solitude- in the house was loneliness- except for her
pen and books and movies- there were ways to succeed
but they seemed beyond her- because the road offered
the least resistance- and it's absurd to expect someone
to go the other way- all the time- she doesn't go to
church- she doesn't feel connection there- but
isolation- isolation is everywhere- it is the only reality-
it is the ocean around her- filed with death and aliens-
dangerous aliens- she seeks romance as an escape- the
story must be true- it was so obvious- there would be
love- if she followed the road- because it fit- and he
was attractive enough- right?-and tall enough-
intelligent enough- and seemed to connect with her-
that wasn't right- exactly- she'd have to compromise, of
course- she knew that- take care of him maybe more
than in an equal partnership- but he was more
successful- better at talking to new people- so, she
could learn to respect him- if it came to it- not that
she relished the introductions- there would be some
judgements- but what else is love for- besides putting
up a fight- a barrier- to all the people who can't
believe in your story- she knew she wasn't the right
girl- not quite thin enough- not quite girly enough- but
he was right there- why else would fate have placed
them so close together as it had?- he didn't have a
choice- they didn't have a choice- these things, how
could they ever happen if people had to choose them-

love is the path of resistance– or it always had been–
she was ready to persevere– ready to make it work– or
anyway, she was curious–

I Found the Butter

It was the last year of Polly's life: less than half a year left, though we didn't know it at the time.

The kids were asleep, and we were sitting in bed, reading. I came to a decision, put my book down, screwed up my courage, and asked, as casually as I could, "So... which kind of husband am I?"

The boundaries of our marriage had become constrictive to her. It took a while to understand what the problem even *was*, but Polly was unhappy and overwhelmed. Our youngest had just turned five and was about to start kindergarten—we were finally exiting Baby Land—but it wasn't enough. Then she found this book, *Fair Play*, and it upended her understanding of the home workload. It gave words to the problem, and a concrete plan of what to do about it.

Among those words was the taxonomy of husbands: Giant Kid, Traditionalist, One-Step-Forward-Two-Steps-Back, More-Than-Most, Where's-The-Butter, etc. The book is trying to snap women out of their resignation, so it's snarky and funny and (not to put too fine a point on it) *not for men*. It even warns readers not to show the book to their husbands. I should know, because after Polly started talking about it, I read it.

"Well...," she hesitated. You're not supposed to tell your husband which kind he is, either. I get it—this whole area is fraught and it's easy to get defensive.

I'd had my share of defensiveness. I'd gone my whole life with a certain story in my head—I'm one of the *good* men. I've always been told this by women, as long as I can remember, even by Polly. Sometimes the praise can get a little silly: boomer women in particular, if they see a man changing a diaper or wearing a baby in a sling, treat him like a goddamn war hero.

It must have gone to my head. In the taxonomy of husbands I was *obviously* a More-Than-Most, right? Right...?

Polly was never one to pull her punches, so she told me straight out: "You're a Where's-The-Butter." *Ouch.*

Where's-the-Butter comes from a classic cartoon, where a man stares into a butter-filled refrigerator and asks, "Hon, where's the butter?" A Where's-The-Butter husband is competent at work (maybe even excellent), but useless at home. Which puts me in mind of the equally classic Universal Cartoon Caption: "Christ, what an asshole."

The problem snuck up on us, and it was compounded by two related factors.

One factor was that I'm great with computers, but... not much else. I combine two stereotypes of the widowed: I couldn't cook (classic widower) and I couldn't fix anything around the house (classic widow). Polly was the opposite—outside of computers, she was good at *everything*.

The other factor was the subtle trap of the stay-at-home-mom. If both partners are working full-time, it's pretty clear (from the outside at least) when things aren't 50/50. The wife doing 90% of the housework and childcare while also working full-time is objectively unfair (and yet it's pervasive).

For the stay-at-home-mom, though, the boundary line is much less clear. And the line *moves*. When we first got married it seemed like a simple break-down: I go to work, Polly makes art and dinner (and I do the dishes). But then we had a kid. And another. And another. And then they started going to school. While Polly's workload grew exponentially, I just kept going to work, where my workload grew (at best) linearly with a promotion every now and then.

Polly was also determined to be a super-wife and super-mom. When someone is that good at what they do, things just seem to…happen. It got to where I couldn't even see it. Of course my ignorance was biased toward my own lazy self-interest. Or to mangle a famous quote, "It is difficult to get a man to understand something, when his wife is doing all the housework."

So after we got done arguing, we sat down with the *Fair Play* cards. Each card is a task that has to get done, like Calendar Keeper, Auto, Meals, School Forms, even Returns & Store Credits. The cards don't have point values to indicate how much time they take up. The idea is that they show how many "balls in the air" we have going on. In a deliberate omission, there is no card for Day Job, though Polly threw me a bone and made me one.

That one extra card didn't make a bit of difference. We divvied up the cards based on how things currently were at the time. I had a few (maybe… More Than Most?). Polly had a giant pile. Oh. That's why she was overwhelmed.

We sorted through the cards to see what I could take

on. Well, I could take on Auto surely. (Which means all the car things: keeping them both gassed up, making sure they get taken in for service, taxes, all of it.)

I could also take on Weekend Meals. (Which means all the meal things: from deciding what to eat to buying the food to cooking it.) If it took me two hours to fumble through making a simple dinner, well, there was time on the weekends. Polly made sure to leave the kitchen entirely and sit on her hands. If I was going to do this, I had to screw it up on my own. We had to accept some not very great meals for a while.

As I got into the swing of it (and I saw the palpable relief in Polly's demeanor), we started to wonder what else I could take on. Here, fix this doorknob (10x the time Polly would have taken, but she didn't have to do it). Here, take School Forms for the elementary kids. Maybe we could start swapping cards that stretch us both, like she could take Electronics & IT for a month while I took Home Maintenance. It's surprising, but *Fair Play* is not a zero-sum game. More work actually felt... empowering?

Look, there's the butter. No, no over there. No, your other left. Up a bit. You're getting warmer. Use your eyes. Look!

We had about five months under the new scheme. And it was *working*. Polly was happy. The air was just beginning to push up under her wings. She was taking off...

And then the blood clot took her from us. Our time had run out. In hindsight, those months before she died feel like nothing so much as *training*. Now I have *all* the cards.

Fair Play taught Polly to stop being an unsustainable super-mom, and it taught me to step up. It articulated so many good reasons to start this process, but it left out a crucial, if unimaginable, reason: What if my wife were to die? What will happen when she's not there to do All The Things?

I'm now usually the only dad on the group texts coordinating kid activities. Even here, in liberal-ass Boulder, I'm one of very few men at school functions. If I want to arrange a playdate, who do I email? The kid's mom. Why? Women seem to always be the ones who initiate change in their marriages. Why? Why wasn't I the one see this problem and take the initiative? Why wasn't I the one to pitch *Fair Play* to my wife? Why wasn't I using my eyes to *look?* Why wasn't I the one to say, "Polly, you seem overwhelmed. What can I do?"

In order to become a better husband, I had to let go of whether I was a good one. I wasn't, in fact, a More-Than-Most. More-Than-*Some*, perhaps, but how is that relevant when there's work to be done? The bar for men is low, too low. We can do better.

Polly started this process at basically the last second. I'm proud of what we did together—we redrew the boundaries of our marriage! How many couples can say that? Though I'm ashamed it took me so long to see the problem. I wish I'd had the sense to see it earlier, so that we would have had more time with the new boundaries before we ran out of time, before Polly crossed that final boundary and was lost to me.

It took a while, it took a lot of pointing and coaching and patience, but that was the year when I *finally* found the butter.

—time is the thing—

time is the thing.: i do not have— i have in abundance— i worry about— we share well— life is defined by— that is before you— that draws out like a knife— that i am wasting— killing— giving— that has shifted— that bears down— that births the baby— wakes the baby— changes everything— reveals all— turns all into dust— gives life meaning— narrative— memory— hope— that remains— blank— untouched— ineffable— gives the life to eternity— molds planets, stars, galaxies— draws wrinkles across my skin— slows the healing of muscles— walks through death— gloomy afternoons— and glorious triumphs— that shall pass— and pass everything— you cannot keep— or buy— or fool though we try try try again— that shapes culture— language— we cannot worry about— i cannot bear to mark the passage of— i don't really understand mathematically— that will rescue me

from my frustrations but not from myself– or, perhaps,
it will cease to hold me– and that will be my end–

Widowest?

widow (n):   a woman who has
lost her husband by
death.

widower (n):   a man who has lost
his wife by death.

widowest (n):   TBD

Then he found a hot returned Peace Corps Volunteer widow artist with kids who weren't spoiled monsters: the full Venn diagram. In a surprising twist, she even had the same name. (Funny story: they met when he texted her about a receipt sent to his late wife's email.) They married and (somehow) blended their families, avoiding the usual pitfalls of step-mothers and step-fathers. There were a lot of *Brady Bunch* jokes. They loved each other and their children with all their hearts, but allowed space for their first, original loves.

They became a *widowest*—a married widow and widower.

Or...

He was sleeping soundly when Sam Beckett Leaped into him in the early morning of October 23, 2022.

This might seem surprising since originally Beckett's experiment was "time travel within his own lifetime," but after the *Quantum Leap* series finale we learned that Sam could control his own Leaps and instead of finally going home *chose to continue Leaping*. He became unbound to his own lifetime and began ranging outside of it, including into the future.

Without Al or Ziggy to help him, Sam had to use his intuition, aided by the "swiss-cheese" mingling of memories of who he'd Leaped into. He knew there was a wife upstairs who was recovering from outpatient surgery. Maybe that had something to do with why he was here?

He rushed upstairs and found her sleeping in bed. She awoke when he entered and complained about shortness of breath. Among Sam's many doctorates (quantum physics, archaeology, chemistry, and others), he was an M.D. Upon examining her he quickly realized that she was developing a blood clot and that time was of the essence. He called 911 for an ambulance, which arrived quickly and rushed her to the emergency room. The doctors gave her blood thinner, and she was ok. Their family was going to be ok.

Time to go. Blue light synthesizer blast.

While the Leapee *remembered* what had happened (swiss-cheese memory mingling, remember?), he never understood *why* he did what he did. It was the closest thing to a miracle either he or and his wife had ever experienced. But she was alive, and that's what mattered.

As time went on, he became preoccupied with what very nearly happened. He had intense imaginings (or were they memories?) of finding his wife's body, of writing the eulogy, of grief, of having to keep it together for the kids.

These parallel memories were horrifying, but tempered by the fact that his wife was alive. He became a *widowest*, one who has narrowly dodged becoming a widow(er) and determined to love their spouse to the fullest.

Or…

After a time, he remarried a kind woman with grown kids. She wasn't what he expected at all, but she was what he needed. He was reminded that was how it was with his first wife originally.

And then she got cancer and had six months to live.

In some ways the advance notice was better this time around. But he still had to watch her waste away. He still held her body at the end, just like before.

Is there a word for someone who has survived multiple spouses? The word is *widowest*.

Or…

After several years of loneliness, desperation drove him to marry the first available woman to cross his path. And she was *awful*. She drove a wedge between him and the kids, she alienated his first wife's family, she caused drama with his own family. Desperate to please her, he lasered off his copy of his first wife's tattoo (the new wife didn't like reminders of the old wife). He put away the rings from the first marriage in a little box, which disappeared one day under questionable circumstances. And who knows what happened to that joke shirt.

He was stuck, unable to figure out whether to show his loyalty to his new wife or to his children, a true *Kobayashi Maru*. He told himself that this was better than being alone, but it wasn't. His new wife was displacing what really mattered—his kids and family.

Widowest is the dark next step of being a widower, where you ceaselessly attempt to fill the infinite hole in your heart with whatever you can get, whether it's good or bad.

Or...

After an initial burst of activity, he ran out of energy to live life. He neglected his kids, not caring if they got dressed or went to school. He neglected work, and was eventually, reluctantly, fired. He drank and slept and cried and moped. Life insurance and savings allowed things to coast for a time, but that finally ran out. The house became a cob-webby shrine to his wife, in which nothing could change.

He'd gone full Havisham and become a *widowest*—one

who is more than a widower, crushed by grief and despair, unable to live.

Or…

He finds himself preoccupied with his wife of the alternative world where he had died, and she the widow. Is she strong? Does she comfort the kids? Does she gasp for breath in fear that the grief will crush her? Does she fear for the future? Does she keep her shit together? Does she remarry? Her strength is a model to him; he knows if she can make it then he can, too.

Does she find herself preoccupied with him, in the alternate world where she had died and he the widower? Is he an example to her? Does she see the dream of herself that he dreams and is it a source of strength for her? Who is dreaming of whom? Who has died?

This is the swirl of identity, ego unmoored, the widow's tempest, the *widowest*.

Or…

He knew that he couldn't raise his kids to be non-broken people if he himself was broken. You can't fake this.

He knew that becoming romantically involved again was a distraction. He had to learn to find meaning and vision in his life without a woman to provide it. Living without the mythology of romance is the last atheism.

It took time, and there was deep sadness, but he lived his life and loved his kids and while there was a hole in their hearts, they *lived*. He knew this was the best way to honor his wife's memory, even though it was the hardest path.

In this he became a *widowest*—one who has transcended grief and embraced life, despite its fragility and brevity.

—now we will—

i came across an old poem just now— from my sestina period— it makes me want to write a sestina for you— bones, snowflakes, flowers, vows, will, together— sequins a-sparkle and eyes damp as snowflakes, melted by the hot of skin as we stand together, barely we remember to breathe barely we remember our vows, forever mocked by the darkness in the shadow of bones, trembling gently moved through the numb emotions we are flowers, a life together a united force committed now we will—

Notes

Polly's chapters are mostly taken from the hand-written journal she kept from 2010 to 2022, with a smattering from sketchbooks and computer journaling.

To keep the feel of her journal, Polly's chapters are rendered with "Pollys1st," a custom font she made out of her handwriting. I've kept the spacing the same, and edited it very little. While she typically didn't begin a sentence with a dash, the chapter titles begin that way as they're typically pulled from within a sentence. It also preserves the sense of having found the entry buried in the surrounding dashed text.

Her entries are undated with no paragraph breaks— just one gigantic run-on sentence. Figuring out where one entry ends, the next one begins, and when it all happened is tricky and depends on a lot of context. In some sense I may be the only person with enough context to figure out what she's referring to at any given moment.

Her journals were such an unexpected gift. Polly lives on in her words.

Foreword

The mosaic pictured here (and on the cover) is a piece Polly made for my mom. We were settled in Boulder, with only a dog and no kids, and made a road trip to Baton Rouge for Christmas. I worked remotely for some of it, and Polly had time on her hands. My mom suggested she do something about an unsightly wooden panel in the carport, expecting Polly to paint it or something. Instead, she came up with this four-foot square mosaic that hung on the wood panel. I think she may have been trying to impress her future mother-in-law.

Widower?

Obituary published on Dec 1, 2022 in Boulder, Colorado's The Daily Camera.

The self-portrait (from Polly's MFA period) is painted wood, with painted plastic nailed into it. I find the overlaid images (skeleton, lungs, heart) haunting.

—the ultimate test of one's values—

Written maybe a month before she died. I've heard of people laughing and crying at the same time, but never experienced it until I read this.

Pictured here are custom tissue boxes she made for our house, which match the painted wall pattern in our bedroom (shown later).

The Vestments of My Office

We loved Lord of the Rings, so it's not lost on me that wearing a ring on a chain parallels Frodo. I'm not sure what to make of that metaphor. Do I need to cast the ring "back in the fiery chasm from whence it came"? At the last, Frodo was unable to do it—will I?

Shown here is another self-portrait from Polly's MFA period. In person, you can see that the doves are suspended pieces of paper inside avocado shells attached to the painting.

—what makes hope courageous—

Written after learning that her friend's father had died while they were Nordic skiing. She's speaking from experience, having lost her mother when she was 18. But now it feels like she's writing it to us about herself.

The painting shown here is from Polly's minotaur series in college.

Bad Ass Mother

Eulogy I gave at her memorial service on Dec 11, 2022. This phrase is hers—she had it on her iPad cover and was in the process of making shirts with it for her friends.

The superhero portrait here is from the photo party that we crashed.

—sestina—

Ses·ti·na (*noun*): A fixed verse form consisting of six stanzas of six lines each, normally followed by a three-line "envoi." The words that end each line of the first stanza are used as line endings in each of the following stanzas, rotated in a set pattern.

To go with the sestina is one of Polly's college poem paintings.

Three Haunted Houses

There's more than one kind of ghost. I told a version of this at Story Collective in April, 2024.

The piece pictured here, titled "Home," is a 4-foot circle showing the Flatirons of Boulder, CO that Polly did for a show called "What Made You Start Again" at the Dairy Center for the Arts. Inside the piece is a micro-controller board that fluctuates lights behind the image in and out. It's timed to Polly's breathing and makes the whole piece seem alive and comforting.

—cabin fever—

The poem and Polly's description of it were written after the family cabin was sold, sometime in 2020. The final section is from a computer document a few years earlier in 2018, one of very few with an actual title, which I used for this chapter's title.

Pictured here is a watercolor Polly did as part of a birthday present to me.

Parting Pro

A "found poem," of phrases people would often say, snippets from websites. Parting Pro, by the way, is a real thing. Visit https://www.partingpro.com/ to find out how to "launch and scale your online cremation business and dominate your market."

Pictured here is a painting Polly did that includes the kids' handprints (a recurring theme with the house art).

—something helpful—

Written for Polly's niece. I don't know if she ever sent it, or what the occasion was for.

The stuffed animals are from an installation Polly did in college called "Preshes" that included custom-made, bizarre/cute stuffed animals. These three she made for brother's kids, Kenya, Thorin, and Mollie.

Sometimes A Man Is An Island

This is what it feels like.

Pictured here is a painting Polly did for me when I got my first job after getting back from Peace Corps. My desk was far from a window, so she painted me one. I've brought this with me from job to job ever since.

—line dancing—

Written in 2007 while Polly was in Peace Corps Philippines.

The painting here (featuring Polly and two fellow Peace Corps volunteers) is from a photo I took at a wedding in the Philippines.

Trigger Finger

I broke my finger in a bizarre water-skiing accident. You can't make this stuff up. While under anesthesia I didn't actually have any visions, but I did sob uncontrollably when coming out of it. It was like being drunk on grief.

I told a version of this at Story Collective in October, 2024.

Pictured here is some of Polly's custom wall painting in our house, from Peggy and Hazel's room.

—birth question—

Written while she was pregnant with our first child, sometime in 2011.

For each of her three pregnancies Polly made a cast of her belly, trying to wait as late as possible (and get a big belly) without running the risk of accidentally having the baby early and missing the chance to make the cast. She was so big that she couldn't quite do all of it herself, so I helped out for the parts she couldn't reach. Then, months after the birth and when she felt recovered and ready, she would mount the cast and paint it.

Soledad

So·le·dad (*feminine noun*): From the Spanish. Solitude, loneliness.

Shown here is a picture collage of baby Peggy. We made one of these for each kid, right around two-and-a-half to three months old. We'd set the baby up in a little bouncy chair under some lights, and take hundreds of photos, trying to capture as many expressions as possible. (If you wait long enough and the baby gets bored, you start to get some interesting poses!) Then we chose the best ones, and Polly took the best nine and arranged them in Photoshop.

—i wondered how i could love you—

These passages were scattered across the years of her journal, but I gathered them together because it shows the depth of her bond for our kids. It was fierce.

Shown here is a photo-trace she did that was used in our 2017 Christmas card, which was styled after a coloring book.

The Widow-er

I've probably exhausted the quota on "widow" wordplay with this book.

As for the early season one version of the Nerd's Catechism ("a time travel experiment that went ... a little caca"), we must pass over it in silence.

Shown here is another of Polly's college era poem paintings, which pairs with the minotaur piece.

—which winter will be the last—

Her last entry. Probably written the evening of Oct 16, 2022, the night before her surgery.

Shown here is another of her house wall paintings.

Do Not Go to the Altar of Vanity

Letter sent to Boulder, Colorado's The Daily Camera just after the first anniversary of Polly's death.

Shown here are a few of the ceramic cake pedestals Polly made for our wedding to hold the various wedding cakes (one per table).

—v secret—

One of very few computer documents called something other than "Untitled." I find her list of physical flaws amusing, because that stuff didn't really matter to me. As we got older, I found her more and more beautiful.

Shown here is a painting Polly did in high school.

Wings and Horns

A letter I wrote to the comic book Saga, which they published in issue #67.

Saga's "lettercol" culture is quite different from the typical comic book, which is mostly just fan-boy gushing. But something about Saga's story invites confessional letters, stories of pain, people writing from prison (!), LGBTQ folks appreciating being "seen," etc. My letter connecting the protagonist's story of loss to my own fit right in.

Shown here is a flying pig Polly made with the kids during COVID. The face is from a sketch three-year-old Cary did.

—dear amy—

We used to read the Dear Amy newspaper column aloud each morning. One of them clearly bugged her enough that she wrote out a response. I don't know if she sent it in, but if she did it never showed up in the column.

Shown here is a heating panel from the girls' room that Polly painted. The butterfly pairs with another super happy caterpillar elsewhere.

Half-Double Grieving

The grief energy has to go somewhere. Polly has provided me with lots of projects to finish.

Shown here is the crochet hexagon blanket that she made for Hazel that I hope to replicate for Cary.

—imagine a hallway—

I remember Polly trying to describe this one to me. I'm not sure why she never made it, but I have a vivid image of the faces and hands bobbing up and down. What an installation piece this would have been.

An early take on this idea was a piece she did with little paper hands that would flutter in the breeze. It actually sold at a show. I can't seem to find any photos of it, though.

Shown here are the custom stair risers she made using the kids' handprints. Also note the industrial-chic kids height chart off to the side.

Polly's Reading List

I wrote this just a few days after she died and sent it out to the email list. She was incredibly well read, so this list should really be pages and pages long.

It's a little on-the-nose, isn't it, that the last book she read was Life Is Hard.

Shown here is Polly's elaborate wall pattern she did for our bedroom (echoed in the custom tissue boxes shown earlier).

—the prom—

Written in 2007 while she was in Peace Corps. What she leaves out is that "heating water to bathe" using the broken light socket is done with what we called the "widowmaker," a 220V electrical heating coil that you immersed *directly into the water.*

Pictured here is one of Polly's lightshades she made for the house.

Taking Back the Lie Dream

I had a half-waking dream, sort of a vision, where the devil showed me that fateful morning. Our house was cut in half like a doll's house, or a Wes Anderson movie, and I could see the kids asleep in bed, Polly on the floor, and me in the bathroom. This piece is an attempt to wrest back control of that "lie dream."

Shown here is a formerly mundane wooden chest that Polly painted and made memorable.

—ways to kill time—

Written in 2007. Making headway in Peace Corps is hard. The combination of her own introversion plus the struggle to convince the teachers that art was valuable made things extra hard.

The photo here is of a prototype chair Polly made. It uses a clever series of cuts in the wood to create the accordion backing. She was exploring using industrial plumbing pipe for furniture and made Cary's bed, the dining table, and benches in a similar fashion.

All You Pollies

Polly is a pretty unusual name, so it's surprising to get so many emails for all these other Pollies. Are they all old and don't know how to use email?

Shown here is a quilt Polly made out of our old shirts, including lots of custom shirts she had made.

—the struggle—

Written sometime in 2020 or 2021. The "failure" she mentions is her internalized sense of failing at Peace Corps. The "ordinary path" is our seemingly conventional breadwinner/SAHM lifestyle. But even within the ordinary, Polly was subverting the institution from within and making it her own. She was no "tradwife."

Shown here is the wall from Cary's room with its custom wall pattern and painted wall heater.

I Still Dream of Krypton

Channeling Polly, I want to make a shirt with a Superman symbol on the front, and "I Still Dream of Krypton..." in green lettering on the back. It would be a way to publicly remember her without making everyone uncomfortable.

Shown here is a mud painting Polly made while in Peace Corps out of a photo of us kissing.

—my mind is alive—

I had this whole plan to go to a nice restaurant and get down on my knee and propose in front of God and everybody. I had the ring box in my pocket, and I was nervous and fidgety. The restaurant wasn't as nice as I thought it would be, and there were loud TVs on all the walls. Ultimately I chickened out until we got back to our apartment and I brought out the box and opened it up and said the words. I even forgot to get down on my knee. She said yes.

Shown here is a piece Polly did for the first show she was in after we got back to the States. We weren't married yet, but she was clearly thinking about marriage. And also how her mother wouldn't be at our wedding. The embroidered words at the bottom of the veil read:

let us pause for a moment of reflection

on the memory of those who are no longer with us

The Butt-Dial of Destiny

Neal Stephenson's Cryptonomicon measures travel in the Philippines in terms of "Lewis and Clark Days." I can't think of a better description.

Shown here is an MFA-era painting Polly did.

—christmas was hot this year—

An email Polly sent in 2008 during our time in Peace Corps Philippines. She eventually got her vengeance and taught me how to ski at A-Basin, which is not exactly a beginner's resort. It was terrifying.

Pictured here are the mix-CDs she made for me while we were dating. The CD on the bottom right is better thought of as an album she made, singing with her acoustic guitar into her MacBook in her tin-roof shack at the top of a rice-terrace in the mountains of northern Luzon.

Than Never To Have

In today's issue of Marvel's "What If...?" we answer the question: what if I were an even bigger jackass than I actually am? In the throes of grief, it's tempting to want to toss it all out. What if I hadn't joined my life to someone fated to die? Maybe I would be happier if I'd broken it off with Polly before it went too far. (In real life, her marriage pitch was very convincing. I never came close to breaking up with her.) I'm not convinced I would be happier in that timeline, though. Human psychology seems capable of enduring any amount of pain if there's the right motivation, the right purpose. I think the purposelessness of Alternate Me is far worse.

Shown here is a cabinet from our kitchen. Polly got tired of the kids (and sometimes me) asking what was for dinner, so she had this printed up on adhesive vinyl.

—married—

Probably written the night of our wedding in 2010. Though knowing Polly, she probably wrote the anxious sequence of words the night before, and then "I am now married" after it was done.

Pictured here is Polly showing off the wedding dress she made. She enjoyed acting as if our photo shoot was for a fashion magazine.

For the Newlyweds

I went to a wedding for one of Polly's nieces. They had a "give us advice!" box with index cards and pens. What can a fresh widower possibly say to newlyweds? I skipped the index cards, went home, and this came out. I toyed with mailing it to them, but in the end I kept it to myself. They should be allowed to experience the early days of their new marriage unburdened with thoughts of their (far off?) deaths.

Shown here are the cake toppers Polly made for our wedding, to go with the cake pedestals shown earlier. Half the toppers are of characters Polly designed, and the other half are famous (to me) nerd couples. I particularly like the felt machine guns held by Kyle Reese and Sarah Conner.

—love is the path of resistance—

Polly often wrote about herself in the third person. Here she is imagining herself back in the Philippines, looking at our (then) new relationship through the eyes of someone ten plus years into marriage. At the time we were entering into a rocky period where we were renegotiating how we did things (housework, how we argued, clearing out built-up resentments, what if she treated making art like a part-time job). She loved me enough to "persevere" through all of it.

Shown here is the wall and sliding mirror of Polly's bathroom remodel, one of her last projects.

I Found The Butter

Being a dumbass, overly literal engineer is cute until it's not.

Shown here is a close-up of one of Polly's wall patterns in our house.

—time is the thing—

This was in a corner of one of her sketchbooks, so it's unclear when it was written. Though the references to the baby make me think it was not that long after our first was born in 2011.

Shown here is another of Polly's wall patterns in our house.

Widowest?

Since this is a book, the pull of narrative tropes is very strong. You're expecting a Lifetime Channel movie ending where the widow whose husband fell from a horse meets up with the widower whose wife died in childbirth, and they get their giant pile of kids together and happily run the farm ever after. I don't have that ending for you. As Polly said, "life is not a fiction and does not obey its laws—" These are the possible paths. I don't know which way it's going to go. Part of the madness of grief is that I give the Quantum Leap ending a non-zero probability.

Shown here is a painting Polly did from a photo of me holding fake bananas up to my ears and pretending I couldn't hear her. It was originally part of a triptych where she painted the photo in three different styles, but the other two have been lost.

—now we will—

It's unclear if the sestina she sketched out here led to the one earlier in this book. The word list is different, but the timing is about right.

Shown here is a painting Polly did for the first show she was in after getting back to the States. The dead bird and her hands holding the rock make me think of Polly's grief over her mother, and what it's like to carry grief.

Notes

Shown here is a flush-to-the-wall computer desk and plumbing-piping bench that Polly made.

Salamats

In Tagalog, the national language of the Philippines, *maraming salamat* means "thank you very much." Here are my salamats.

Maraming salamat sa Katheryn Lumsden, Rebecca Dickson, and Nathan Pieplow. Katheryn in particular became a kind of pseudo-agent, helping me with the process of what to do with this thing I'd written. At some point I realized that you all weren't just "humoring the widower." Or if you are, it would be really socially awkward to back out now.

Maraming salamat sa Lizzie Parsons and Katie Horney for running (and repeatedly letting me participate in) Story Collective Boulder. Reading my pieces live in front of an audience was terrifying, exhilarating, and cathartic. The feedback I got from you and the audience was crucial to the formation of this book.

Maraming salamat sa Wes Magyar and Mark Sampson for your excellent art documentation photography of Polly's various works.

Maraming salamat sa the wonderful Diane Windsor of Motina Books for taking a chance on this strange book and helping me to fulfill Polly's last dream.

Maraming salamat sa Polly's friends, Mark Pergola, Rachel Doniger, Brandi Lippman, Mary Pat LaMair, Amy Slaymaker, Betsy Johson, and Bonnie Draina, who passed the golden baton of their friendship with Polly on to me.

Maraming salamat sa Polly's family, the Gates': Bart, Rudd, Joel, Kristi, Leah, Kenya, Hadassah, Thorin, Adli, and Mollie. I married in, and you've let me stay in. It means so much to me.

Maraming salamat sa my family: my mom Barbara Tarleton, my dad and stepmom Mike and Donis Simmons, and my sister Sarah Simmons. When Polly died they dropped everything to come be with us, and have since had the patience and love to let me go through this in my own way.

Finally, *maraming salamat sa* my kids, Peggy Jo, Hazel Maude, and Cary Jay: of all my collaborations with Polly, our best.

About the Authors

Aaron Michael Simmons (1977-)

Originally from Baton Rouge, Louisiana, though you can't tell it from his accent. Also the author at 15 of *Surface Thoughts*, a weird little novella about two telepathic brothers fighting over a girl. It was one of those child prodigy moments that don't go anywhere—it turns out it's much easier to write code than meaningful words.

He moved to Boulder, Colorado after a stint as an IT volunteer in Peace Corps Philippines (2006-2008) and married Polly Gates in 2010.

Lately the sole father of three. Writes computer software for a living, and sometimes words.

Polly Jo Gates Simmons (1979-2022)

Raised in Lakewood, Colorado. Earned a BA and MFA from CU Boulder. Served as an education volunteer in Peace Corps Philippines (2006-2008). Married Aaron Simmons in 2010.

She was fully and confidently herself. She didn't sleepwalk through life—the word everyone uses to describe her is "intentional."

An avid diarist, her journal entries fuel this book. She wanted to be a writer, but she didn't realize she already was.

An amazing mother, better than she understood herself to be.

Polly, we carry you with us.